AM I DOING IT RIGHT?

AM I DOING IT RIGHT?

Conversations with Team Leaders & Broker Owners Who Are **KILLING IT**

CHRISTINE ANDREASEN
& AARON HENDON

BMD Publishing

Am I Doing It Right? Conversations with Team Leaders & Broker Owners Who Are Killing It

Copyright © 2023 Christine Andreasen & Aaron Hendon

BMD Publishing
All Rights Reserved

ISBN # 979-8367114102

BMDPublishing@MarketDominationLLC.com
www.MarketDominationLLC.com

BMD Publishing CEO: Seth Greene
Graphic Design: Kristin Williams

Sale of this book without a front cover may be unauthorized. If this book is coverless, it may have been reported to the publisher as "unsold or destroyed" and neither the author nor the publisher has received payment for it.

No part of this publication may be reproduced, stored in a retrieval system, or transmitted in any form or by any means, electronic, mechanical, photocopying, recording, or otherwise, without the prior written permission of the Publisher. Requests to the Publisher for permission should be sent to BMD Publishing, 5888 Main Street, Suite 200, Williamsville, NY 14221.

Printed in the United States of America.

ACKNOWLEDGMENTS

Christine:
What fun this adventure this has been! Real Estate, the podcast, this book and this thing called life.

Aaron and I both love finding ways we can contribute and how we can empower other leaders. Really we love to contribute to anyone, anywhere & always.

I'm grateful for many people who have stood for me so ferociously.

Aaron, thanks for your continued partnership and love over the decades! Thanks for causing our team to exist.

I owe many thanks to Brian, my partner, who puts up with my hyper mind and crazy ideas, 24/7. Thanks, Brian for loving me and my mind unconditionally.

I appreciate all our clients who trust us with their business, their families and their friends and made all this success possible.

Werner Ehrhardt, you transformed my life in 1979 and it's never been the same. I love you.

Kelly Tadlock, thanks for being my coach, and teaching me how to do less and be more and stay true to the magic that I am. Everything changed the day the Universe sent you to me. I love you.

And a huge shout-out to the agents at Christine & Company! You all are a rare breed of exceptional people and I'm honored to be with you.

I am blessed.

Aaron:
This has been a privilege.

I love training people and love helping people discover and remove whatever is in their way. But that would never be possible for me if I hadn't had amazing teachers and trainers for my whole life. I didn't wake up like this – I was made through the hard work of an endless stream of committed human beings.

From Jan Groover, whose critical voice never leaves my head, to the men and women who lead the Landmark Forum, who never ever listened to me as anything but a possibility, my life is function of those that were committed that I show up bigger than I thought I could, even when my own commitment wavered.

My wife and children have trained me to listen and to lead with love – something my high D, New York upbringing does not leave me suited for.

And in this particular endeavor, my partner Christine Andreasen, who was willing to be my teacher in all things real estate and has quite literally transformed my life from a month-to-month existence to a millionaire, I owe everything.

TABLE OF CONTENTS

Acknowledgments iii
Meet Christine & Aaron 1
Foreword: Are We Doing It Right? 5
Introduction: The Big Idea 11

1. Chris Angell 25
2. Cambria & Robert Henry 37
3. Jeff Willmore 51
4. Jesse Zagorsky 63
5. Lisa Maysonet 85
6. Sarah Richardson 97
7. Nick Good 109
8. Tara Stone 129
9. Jami Amidon 151
10. Brett Rosenthal 169
11. Patricia Love 185
12. Ryan Garson 197

Now What? 211

MEET CHRISTINE & AARON

Before you hear from all the knowledgeable professionals (and really interesting people) who will be sharing their insights with you in the upcoming chapters, let's give you some insight into us. How did we get into this amazing profession, how did we form our partnership, and what led us to this book? It's been an interesting journey for both of us.

Christine's Story

I got into real estate in 1996 in Utah. I was also doing some speaking for a company called Landmark Worldwide. I had sold a grand total of ONE home when a man saw me speaking and told me I should be a keynote speaker in the real estate industry. After selling one home. He took me to Hilton Head to watch him speak to a group of agents, and sell them a high-priced coaching package. I was smitten, and ended up being a keynote speaker for 10 years.

First of all, I'm very transparent, and I apologize ahead of time if this is TMI, but in 2007, my mom was diagnosed with terminal cancer and given four weeks to live. I put my life on hold and went back and forth from Seattle to Florida to be with her. Four weeks turned into 18 months. During that time, I spent all my savings and cashed out my 401(k), which I would do all over again if I had to. I knew when the time came and I went back to work, I'd be fine. I lost her the summer of 2008,

I went back to work in September, and we all know what happened that October.

The company I was working for went under, owing me tens of thousands of dollars. So, there I was, with no job, no money, owning three houses that were worth less than what I owed on them. Everyone was abandoning the real estate industry, and I decided to dive back in. As Warren Buffett says, "Be greedy when others are fearful, and fearful when others are greedy." I made next to no money, got deeper in debt to the IRS, and lost two of my homes. Eventually, after fighting like hell, got the bank to modify my loan for the home I still have, and began making some money, and finally, I was back in the black.

But I did all this on my own, and I realized I couldn't keep up that pace. Then in 2013, Aaron reconnected with me (we had known each other for 20 years at Landmark) and said, "I'm getting into real estate. I'm going to be on your team." I said, "I don't have a team," and he replied, "You do now."

Today there are 20 people on that team and it's growing all the time.

Aaron's Story

I'm originally from New York. I graduated from art school with a Bachelor of Fine Arts, which basically made me eligible to work in food service anywhere in the country.

I moved to Albuquerque, New Mexico with my girlfriend, and began waiting tables. Again, that's what a bachelor of fine arts qualifies you for. But then the baker at the restaurant quit, and I knew how to bake bread, so I did that, and did it pretty well because I won a couple blue ribbons at the state fair for my challah and rye bread, so I decided to open a bakery. Being from New York, I opened a New York bagel shop. In Albuquerque. It was very successful, and I did that for almost 10 years.

Along the way I hired a business coach, who recommended that I do a training with Landmark, which I loved so much I ended up selling my bakery and leading programs for them. As Christine mentioned, that's where we met.

Eventually I left Landmark and got into sales. Everyone around me told me I should go into real estate, which I never thought would be my path, but I made the switch, and then Christine and I partnered up, and we've been kicking butt ever since.

We refer to each other as partners, but it's really Christine's business. That's why it's called Christine & Company. She's Christine, I'm Company. We relate to each other like partners, but she leads the way. What's great for me is in addition to selling, I have the chance to train people again. We're teammates, working together to grow our team.

FOREWORD: ARE WE DOING IT RIGHT?

While we like to think we're special, the truth is we're just like everyone else in a lot of ways. We worry more than we know is good for us. We are harsh, with ourselves and others, even when we know being patient and kind is the smarter option.

We don't think we're alone in these things – after training tens of thousands of people over the last 30 years we're clear most people have a pretty clear picture that shows what they "should do" is all too often not what they "actually do".

So a while back, when our team's performance wasn't meeting our expectations, and it felt like no matter what we tried, nothing worked, we were left with a question – "what are we doing wrong?"

Truth is we were doing ok in production, good enough to be in the top 5 in the brokerage. But we lost what we felt like were too many people and we hated that.

We hated to see people fail, and in an industry with an 87% failure rate, it happened a lot.

One day we were brainstorming, and we decided to do something about it.

Since we already think everyone else is doing better than us (the grass is always greener on our neighbor's lawn) we thought we'd ask them what they do. We wanted to hear what other successful, effective team leaders do, and how they think about their teams and their businesses.

This light-bulb moment changed everything for us.

We started interviewing some of the most successful real estate leaders out there.

Over the course of more than a year we interviewed over 50 top team leaders and broker owners and asked them what they did to get the most of their teams.

What did they do, on a daily basis, to achieve their success? How did they think about their business and their team?

And what we found surprised us.

While the individual practices they used differed a bit, overall, a common thread appeared. They all share a certain philosophy and a particular orientation to their team.

We discovered the operating principles these top-tier leaders use to succeed and have distilled it down here.

This book is the culmination of this research and experience. It's intended to help real estate team leaders and broker owners to reliably empower their agents to perform, produce, and prosper.

Here are three simple principles these successful teams use to unlock their teams' potential. It's an inside look at how they think, operate, and fulfill their mission to make sure their team wins.

If you're a real estate team leader or broker owner, this book is for you! You'll learn how to get the most out of your agents and create an environment that fosters growth, performance, and success.

It's a must-read for any real estate team leader who is looking to go beyond traditional sales training and motivation. This is not about how to get your team to sell two more FSBOs. It's not another book about how to kill it on TikTok or YouTube. It's not about how to sell more homes - although following these principles will have your team sell more homes.

This book is not for you if you're looking for "new" sales tactics. It's not for you if you want recruiting "tips". It's not about quick fixes, or how to double your business in a month through whatever system happens to be popular on Instagram right now.

Speaking of educating people, that's why we did this book. If you're a team leader or brokerage owner, there's a ton of really important information in these interviews. We certainly learned a lot when we had these conversations. We also got a lot of validation.

These professionals, like us, believe there's a better way to lead a team and run a real estate business. A better way to treat your team, and in doing so, grow your business.

Who should read this book? If you want to take your team or your brokerage to another level, you should read this book. If you're not getting what you think you should be getting out of your team or brokerage, you should read this book. There are a lot of people out there who are working really hard, but don't know what they don't know about how to make it easier. There are people running brokerages who aren't getting a revenue share. They aren't getting stock. That's insane. Some of these older, antiquated brokerages don't provide anything, and these agents just don't know what's possible.

You'll also learn this very important point. Your job isn't to sell houses. It isn't even to train your people to sell houses. Your job is to take care of them as human beings, to have them grow and succeed as a human being. Every successful team leader or broker/owner has that as their mission.

This book will lead you toward becoming a better leader. You'll have a better team, you'll be grounded in what works and what doesn't work, and you'll see what are the most effective actions to take and how to make them as effective as possible. Because if you grow people, your business will grow as well.

We are starting with a premise to which you will need stay true:

Your personal and business success is dependent on the growth and success of the agents on your team.

You cannot be here just for you. You must be authentically interested in the success of the people around you.

Said another way, the game we're inviting you to play has two components:
1. Creating a net worth of your choosing by empowering others to create the net worth they choose.
2. Everyone involved is actively fulfilling what matters to them.

Are you someone who makes their living, and whose life is dedicated to, having the people around them succeed? If so, this is a blueprint for you to enjoy the same success as the top in our profession.

It is my hope that inquiring into this will help us, you, and I, make a bigger difference with our teams and our lives.

Quick side note: Nothing we say should be read as "the truth". This is all a possible place to look from and your take on this will likely be more valuable to you than thinking we have an "answer".

At the same time we are suggesting that by implementing the common threads each team leader expressed into your own leadership not only will individual growth be possible but also collective, team success is likely.

If you'd like to connect, mastermind, ask anything, please reach out anytime.

So, if you happen to come up to one of us down the road and say, "I read your book six months ago," we hope you finish that sentence this way: "…and it made a big difference for me. Let me tell you about my success."

Because that's why we're doing this. To make a difference. To empower people. So, let's get started on that.

INTRODUCTION: THE BIG IDEA

Be clear none of the interviews here are "about" this big idea. In fact, a lot of the interviews that follow are about a lot of other aspects of running a team, social media, teams based on REO, lots of different ways to make teams work.

There are a ton of tips, great ideas, different thinking from these brilliant agents.

We've included these all here as a resource for your own "reference brainstorming".

Accountability, Possibility, and Listening: How Top Team Leaders Unlock the Potential of their Teams

There is a place where accountability, possibility, and listening intersect and it is there that we, as team leaders, have a shot at unleashing our teams' potential.

Imagine leading a real estate team where agents feel supported and motivated, work is fun and collaborative, and everyone feels like they are part of something larger.

A team where each agent has created a vision for themselves that is inspiring to them, and they are consistently producing at a high level.

A team where agents not only demand more of themselves than anyone else does but, if they fail to hit their goals, they ask for, and act on, your coaching.

It's possible - with the right mix of accountability, possibility, and listening.

N.B. We are going to be using these three words in a way that you may not be used to seeing them so go slowly here. It is through this intentional use of language we have a shot at creating something beyond what would happen anyway.

The principle here is what Albert Einstein meant when he said, "We can't solve problems by using the same kind of thinking we used when we created them." If we use the same old language, in the same old ways, we are going to get the same old results.

Creating specific use case applications for each of these words will leave you with the opportunity to produce new results.

The importance of accountability

We assert accountability is the access to a successful career as an agent (as it is to a successful life).

Accountability offers us the opportunity to both make and complete promises.

The standard definitions generally refer to the state of being accountable. Accountable then is defined as the state of giving an account, an answer, an explanation.

In ordinary reading it is to answer for, or take responsibility for, one's actions.

This is fine, and we have no argument with this, as far as it goes. But this definition misses a profound opportunity to impact performance.

We suggest looking one step before action. Consider that the act of making promises before acting is the access to living a created life and a key piece of accessing the power of accountability.

Before we landed on the moon, JFK made an impossible promise. Every great mind of the time agreed, the promise to be on the moon by the end of the decade was not possible, it could not be done, the science didn't exist.

But Kennedy's words created a future, that when acted on, created a breakthrough that would not have been possible had he not made the promise.

Ordinary people make promises only when they know they can produce the result. They fear breaking their promises because of the moral implications, because of how it will make them look, or how they will feel.

Extraordinary people understand that promises can be used to help them take actions they wouldn't take if they didn't make that promise.

I like to think about it like the way Batman uses the Bat Hook. Back in the day, Batman, the Adam West version, used to throw his Bat Hook all the way up to the top of the building and then use the rope to pull himself up the building (sometimes even out of quicksand!).

That's the way extraordinary people use promises. They throw them way out there into the future and they use the power of their word to pull them into taking the actions that will fulfill the promise.

Here's why we bring this up: if you look for accountability from the ordinary definitions, we only see the opportunity to account for one's actions. We don't see in it the definition for one to account for one's actions compared to what one promised.

Said even more to the point, if you don't account for one's actions in the presence of the future one was creating, you're just "accounting" for activity.

Without paying any attention to accounting for the way the actions fulfilled the vision, the future, the promise, we are no more likely to achieve it than if we didn't account at all.

While there is a basic utility to say, "We did X and it produced Y", it's missing critical context.

When we say, "I promised X would be fulfilled. And to fulfill X I would take Y actions. In the end I took (or didn't take) Y actions and they fulfilled (or didn't fulfill) X", we presence the world we are looking to create.

We provide context, and we are suggesting this is critical in unleashing performance.

This context allows us to examine results in the light of the future we are fulfilling. We get to look for what was missing in the fulfillment of what matters to us. We are forced to ask what's still needed? And we can celebrate wins inside our fulfilling our word.

With no opportunity to account in this way life becomes one long, never ending stream of activity.

This is what John Wooten was pointing to when said, "Never mistake activity with achievement". It is accountability, when connected to the promise of a future we are out to fulfill, that allows for achievement.

As will become clear as we define the rest of the puzzle, we must define accountability as the opportunity to account for the fulfillment of what one promised to produce in order for us to produce the breakthrough in performance we are looking for.

The guiding principle here is that without this kind of accountability talk is cheap.

When our team knows what they say (promise) matters, they operate with honor for what they said. They become bigger people who continue to expand what they can produce.

Accountability, when defined this way, says what we say and do does matter, and to the degree what we say and do matters, we matter.

Access the power of possibility.

We could devote many, many pages to distinguishing the different meanings one could assign to the word "possibility" but we won't. For this conversation we'll settle on the one that makes a difference for what we are building.

First, let's start here: What we found was every successful team leader took an interest in what the agents on their team wanted for their future.

This might be called their vision. It was sometimes referred to as their personal mission statement. We use the word "calling" on our team (e.g. my calling is all people experience agency in their life.)

In all cases it went well beyond their goals or financial targets.

The questions the team leaders asked were:
- What are the agents on my team fulfilling?
- What inspires them?
- What moves them?
- What are they up to with their lives?
- What matters to them?"

What we mean by possibility is the space in which any, or all, of that could be fulfilled. What we mean by possibility is the future the individual agent is creating for themselves.

You can begin to get a picture of how these fit by connecting our use of accountability here.

Attempts to hold people to account for meeting a target is a top-down phenomenon. Like a factory foreman, assuring each worker makes their quota of widgets.

Absent an inspiring future, a possibility, the conversations starts and stops with, "how many dials, contacts, appointments, etc..."

The opposite of top-down is possibility-based accountability which moves from the ground up. It requires a different skill set of the manager. They are no longer simply making sure the right amount of activity happens (although the right amount of activity still must happen). They are now required to be interested in what each person on the team is up to, what matters to them.

Consider that our lives become more meaningful when we are accountable for what we say our lives are for and the actions we take to fulfill that. The act of accounting for what we've done/not done in the fulfillment of what matters to us is what creates the pathway to fulfillment.

Now the manager can empower each person on the team to look for themselves as to where they are in reference to fulfilling what they said matters to them.

This is what allows the manager to no longer "hold people to account" but allows each person to hold themselves to account.

Not only does the team leader need a different skill set from the ordinary "management" but the agents need something else as well.

Each team member needs the time and guidance to create a future, a possibility that is important to them. This work, the act of creating a personal future that matters, is no small task.

Many effective sales trainings involve having the salesperson uncover the "why" of the consumer. This is a good analogue for the work to be done.

You want the agents connected to a future that matters to them and see their job as the access to the fulfillment of that future. When leaders open this doorway, they are often inspired by their team members and their stories, creating an entirely new future for the individual, the team, and the company.

The two headwinds are:
a) most people don't believe they can create what they want and
b) most team leaders won't take the time to go deep enough

It's in the last piece, listening, that you can find what you need to overcome these.

The act of listening

Where this all comes together is how the manager listens to what is being said.

You might consider that a manager's true role in unlocking the potential of the people on their teams is to be their committed listener.

Committed listening (the kind of listening a committed listener provides) is distinct from ordinary listening.

Ordinary listening is much more likely to be simply hearing. You can hear what people say and not be committed to their fulfilling anything. In fact, that is almost always what's happening. People say things, I hear them say it, and I think, "that would be great", or "we'll see" or "good luck with that".

In that kind of relationship, I, as the person listening, am not committed to anything. I have nothing at stake, it's their promise and it's up to them. Good luck with that, indeed.

In committed listening however, I am a partner. I am in essence, making a promise (I am committing myself) to that person's promise. Now I don't just hear what they say. I inspect it. I care. I check to make sure they have what they need to succeed. I make certain they are not only clear on what actions to take, but they have a clear path to take them.

The whole relationship is a "one voice" kind of thing. The agents' promise IS the managers' promise. In this way the manager is required to listen carefully to what the agent is promising.

In this relationship, the manager's job is not to make sure widgets are made, but to make sure that the person whose promise they are committedly listening to is fulfilling what matters to them.

These are different worlds.

This requires real thought and slowing waaaaaaaay down.

First of all, the promises cannot be just X number of contacts, or $X volume. The promise cannot just be a number.

The promise being listened to is the fulfillment of what matters to the agent. Given my calling, what matters to me is people experience agency, my promises all revolve around empowering people to live independent, autonomous lives, where they have the say about which way their lives go.

Next there's the actions the agent is going to take to fulfill that which they just said matters. This book is an example of that for me. Its intention is to give you (and the agents on your team) more agency.

So the agent is promising to fulfill some possibility that matters to them (for me, it's people experiencing agency in their life). Then there are the actions, that when taken, will forward the fulfillment of that possibility (I will teach 4 first time home buyer classes this month, I will call 10 FSBO and listen for where I might be of service to what they want, I will finish this book to empower team leaders, etc.

Then there are the ways I am going to measure the success.

This cannot be given lip service. It takes an enormous amount of discipline for anybody to listen to anyone for any length of time, much less to listen to what someone says in a way that would leave the listener able to promise the promise of the person speaking.

Consider listening in this way to be a practice.

It cannot be a one time or even occasional thing. It's like drinking enough water during the day, or eating right, or exercising. These are not one-off activities. You don't go to the gym, get buff, and think "now I'm fit for life".

The moment you stop practicing is the moment it all starts to deteriorate. There is no stasis. What's being created by listening is either expanding or contracting.

How accountability, possibility, and listening intersect to create success

The intersection of these three could go something like this:

1. Every team member takes the time to create a possibility, a future, that inspires them, that is important to them, that matters to them. (If you're interested in a free one-hour webinar where your team can work out what their "True North" is, let me know).

2. This is shared publicly, and people become known for the future they are creating. Sharing this is critical – not optional - without the sharing, without the "saying", there is nothing to be accountable for.

3. Standing in the fulfillment of this future, each person works backward to distinguish (and invent) what it took to get there and/or what pathways are available today to create it. What will that world look like? What are the aspects of life that you are going to impact? What steps were taken? What could you do today that would forward this game? What goals were met? What

targets necessarily were fulfilled in the realization of the future?

4. These steps, goals, targets, etc. are created with a committed listener. The manager has the experience and knowledge to brainstorm effective strategies and actions.

5. The team members and committed listeners align on benchmarks and milestones. These will act as guides to determine if sufficient progress is being made. This allows the need for corrections and adjustments to be seen.

This initial conversation is critical. The committed listener must not step over anything they cannot see the team member fulfilling.

If a rocket is off one degree at launch it will miss by miles. If the committed listener can't see the promise being fulfilled based on the actions the team member is willing to take they either need to:
- see to it they take different actions or
- they don't make that promise.

6. Regular check-ins are scheduled between the listener and the team member. This gives the agent the opportunity to account for the actions they took/didn't take and for the results of those actions.

The same principle applies here. While a rocket must have a perfect launch, it also must make constant corrections.

7. Adjustments to existing (and new) plans, strategies, actions, and promises are made based on progress.

The biggest pitfalls in implementation

1. Insufficient time to create the future. Without a future that is inspiring to the individual, there is nothing for anyone to committedly listen for. You're left in the world of making widgets.

2. Not sharing the future. It's critical to understand that the future, the possibility, the team creates does not exist anywhere in reality, yet. It only lives in people speaking it. People speaking about what they are building is the first step in them holding themselves to account for what they are up to.

3. Lack of integrity in listening. Both when initial plans are made, and at each check-in, the committed listener is either listening with integrity, that is, they can see that the promised actions have a high probability of realizing the future (or represent a step on that path), or they are going through the motions. Nothing destroys a team faster than the committed listener giving up, and not saying they did so. If they can't hear the future being fulfilled it is up to them to say so, do something to change that.

4. Insufficient or too infrequent occasions to follow up and adjust/correct plans and actions. This is more important in the beginning of all plans and more important for less experienced agents.

Ready to go?

Every successful team I've interviewed does some version of this, even if they never articulated it this way.

Our job as team leaders is to create an environment, a culture, in which people win. We will only win to the degree to which our people win.

By taking the time to allow each team member to create and share their vision we are talking the talk.

When we committedly listen and allow people to hold themselves to account for its fulfillment, we are walking the walk.

I think you'll find this encourages collaboration and innovation between team members while fostering trust and respect. The result is a team that can achieve more than they ever thought possible.

Any team can unlock their hidden powers and become unstoppable in their pursuit of greatness.

Because the beginning of this process is so important, and se infrequently practiced, I have created a class for our team to find their calling – From Grind to Flow: Uncovering Your Life's True North.

Given everything we discovered is contingent on this being done well, I am happy to offer this to you as my gift – just reach out and we can get something on the books.

CHRIS ANGELL

AARON

It takes a lot for leaders and brokers to crack the code and reap the rewards of success that they couldn't achieve on their own. So, we're starting a new community called RePurpose Beyond the Transaction Let's talk about the purpose of community and what we're building. Then we can begin to hash out the pillars. For now, let's start with the premise. Where are we with the purpose of this community?

CHRIS

The prompt for the premise is, "When blank happens, the world will change." If you use that for yourself and answer that question, you can take your life's work to the next level. What else are we doing with this life beyond the real estate transaction? We want to talk to real estate agents who think like that and want to have that conversation. When agents realize or fulfill the difference they want to make, the world will change.

AARON

The distinction between realize as in fulfill as opposed to realize as in discover is an important one. That's how you have a vision. It needs to be bold and big. Do you really believe the world will change, the war in Ukraine will end, and the polar ice caps will stop melting people realize the difference they want to make in the world? When we talk about "changing the world" the idea seems too big. If I was going to poke holes in your argument, I would go straight to the questions I just asked. When I answered that question, I was thinking of the world of real estate. Real estate is the domain in which we fend for our families, and we engage with our communities, which changes that world. There are realtors who are actively engaged in equity issues and make a direct line between what we do and equity super. I get involved with a domestic violence organization. Our people make every kind of contribution.

CHRIS
That comes back to my point, because you are changing the world outside of just real estate by working with domestic violence. When people realize their mission what they want to change in the world, changes.

AARON
That's great to work it out that way. That's the nature of this community. We must build our teams with other agents who want to have these conversations. I don't know how that is supposed to look, do you? We're engaging with people who are interested in doing in something other than figuring out how to add 350K more to your pipeline in two weeks without cold calling.

CHRIS
There are ways agents show up and behave in their spheres of influence that aren't ways people outside of real estate show up to their spheres. There's some unique nuance to the fact that

real estate is in the background of this conversation, because it's a community of real estate agents or people in the real estate space who show up.

AARON

Say more about that. What do you mean by show up?

CHRIS

There are certain ways real estate agents go about their profession. Even though I'm no longer licensed, I grew up in this industry. I pop by, send newsletters, held pie giveaways, and everything else agents do to stay in contact with their communities that other people in different industries don't do. Other people don't pop by, send newsletters, or give away pies. Other people don't mail handwritten notes. All that engagement is in the background with the community creates an opportunity for me to discuss the difference I want to make in the world with my sphere in my community.

AARON

It's true, no one else pops by or sends newsletters and if they do it doesn't have the same regularity as ours. The nature of our business requires us to be in touch that way because of the infrequency of that conversation. Otherwise, we're not relevant to our clients. Not only are we engaging with people about something that matters to us, but we are developing our community to something larger than having people refer their friends. Maybe your conversation is about building equity or ending domestic violence. We are agents of change, no pun intended.

CHRIS

If an agent wants to make a difference in domestic violence, and they do a pie giveaway for their real estate business, there are different ways they can bring attention to their cause. For example, for every pie given away that day, they could also give a pie away to a woman in temporary housing. It could just be a conversation piece that lets people know this is important to that agent. That champions the hearts of others. When they bring their passion to the conversation, others become interested.

AARON

There are very few people who are going to bring up those issues. Sometimes issues can be polarizing. For example, supporting a political movement might filter out some of your business. If the issue is really important to them, they are probably okay with losing potential customers who don't agree with them. They don't have to do business with everybody, and they don't have to be interested in doing business with everybody. The nature of community is widening the view.

CHRIS

My company is called Groundswell because there is a groundswell that ripples out when I do a pie giveaway. I'm talking to 300 people who come to get pies and now there is an ongoing conversation in my community about the stuff that matters to me. There's an awareness that happens. There's a generational pattern that could end from this conversation. Somebody else may pick up the issue I'm interested in. This is how change happens.

AARON

Having deep conversations is what changes the world. There is no other pathway to that. There is an opportunity for the repurposed community to build and environment and ecosystem, so we can stay true to that. We are empowering each other. The issues that matter to me might be different than the issues important to other agents, but the thing that matters is not the connector, it's where a community comes together and thinks through and investigates that kind of leadership.

The other thing we have been discussing are the pillars. What are the pillars?

CHRIS

There are different ways to think about that. Once there's a premise and the agent knows what kind of changes he wants to make, the world will change. What are the ingredients to make that happen?

AARON

I like the idea of using ingredients as a metaphor because when you bite into cake you know it's made of flour, sugar, and eggs, but you don't know how much of the ingredients are in each bite. You just know if you take the right ingredients in the right proportion and mix them up, it's going to work out. We can take our ingredients, mix them up, and see how they turn out. Then each agent can adjust the ingredients to what makes sense for them.

CHRIS

The ingredients could be the same regardless of the social cause. For example, you would need leadership, or you wouldn't be able to fulfill the difference you were trying to make.

AARON

Without leadership, it's got the potential to be a marketing ploy. If you're not willing to stand for it. So, we need to define leadership. There isn't leadership without action. And so we got to define leadership. We all have a sense of what it means, but it be useful I think for us at some point define it. I don't think today is the day, but I think leadership is one of those things. I would say action, but I don't think there's leadership without action.

CHRIS

Action might be a sub-function of leadership. Communication connection represent enrollment. There is communication that must happen for the work to grow. You're going to have to talk about it for that work to grow.

AARON

You and I have a different definition of enrollment than that of the public. Enrollment usually means registration, but we're talking about enrollment creating something new. Seth Godin talks about enrollment in the world of creating where people must see something for themselves and be willing to act on it. Leadership and enrollment are important here. Vision is also important.

CHRIS

Are enrollment and vision different from leadership?

AARON

It's possible to have a vision without leadership. For example, Putin has leadership qualities, but he lacks vision. One could argue that all autocrats have a vision, but it's a shitty vision.

CHRIS

I understand the difference.

AARON

This is a demonstration of the work we want this community and platform to provide for people. We want them to have a place to work out ideas and engage with others without worrying about producing a finished project. If this is something you're interested in, then this is the community for you. If you don't find this valuable for you in some way, the community is not for you.

CHRIS

Vision holds the cause. If you want to make a difference in the world, you must have a vision of the difference you want to fulfill. I think you must have a vision for the cause and then a plan that gets you to your vision. Leader is the action that gets you to your vision. What is the fourth ingredient that goes with leadership, enrollment, and vision?

AARON

Integrity or authenticity. The mission you're trying to communicate must be authentic to you and have integrity. It should be expressive of who you are, and you should be true to your vision.

CHRIS

Integrity is part of leadership. How you lead should be congruent with your authentic self. It's a distinct part of leadership. We have action and integrity inside of leadership. Leadership is about how I do it, ad enrollment is about how I speak to it and who I speak with.

AARON

How I engage with others is important and I should be engaging them with my vision.

CHRIS

Our three ingredients are leadership, enrollment, and vision. Then each of our ingredients should have four pillars.

AARON

Vision is also connected to purpose and who we are. Purpose is fundamental. Instead of vision, purpose should be a pillar. When I say vision, I mean purpose. It's important to make sure though that you aren't getting things done to check them off a list. There is a little more room around vision.

CHRIS

For me, purpose in the world has a pull to it or a future pull of purpose. The term vision feels aspirational. Purpose feels like it propels me forward. Visions can be untouchable because they're so big. Purpose keeps pulling me through it. Vision is one of the distinctions of purpose. My vision for this community is casual enough that we can play with the topics. It's not a performance. We don't perform for you. You get something or you don't. This is a round table conversation where we discuss ideas we are trying to work out.

AARON

This is not for a seminar or webinar. It's more like a salon. There is a leader to direct, but the leader doesn't know the outcome because there is no specific outcome. They're leading a conversation or an inquiry into various topics, and they have got material to spark conversation in that topic. They aren't teaching what the topic is.

CHRIS

No one here is on a pedestal. It doesn't matter what your GCI is. It doesn't matter how long you've been in the business. All the typical measures of success in real estate, don't apply here. What matters is the willingness to show up with a vision, a purpose, your willingness to lead it, and your willingness to be in dialogue with us and others about it. There is an inquiry that enrollments need. It invites the question and the not knowing.

AARON

Not knowing is a critical space.

CHRIS

If you can't stay open and curious about what you can't see in your blind spot, then you're hamstrung and won't fulfill the difference you want to make. Once we've created the pillars these will become the topics we hold space for. We'll do a series on leadership, one on enrollment, and one on purpose. It becomes a container where we can focus our conversation and where we look. There can be training on the topic or breakout sessions. We won't be training people, people will have breakout sessions to work through their purpose. If someone is stuck on their purpose, we work through that together. We will also have guests who come in and talk about how they are fulfilling the difference they want to make in the world. They'll talk about their purpose and allow others into their community so the others can serve and find their own purpose.

AARON

Engaging in conversation with people in an authentic way makes a difference. It really is outside of the normal realm of how to sell six more houses. Inman Connect is a brilliant platform for that kind of thing. Family reunions and conferences are great, but no one is having real conversations about making a difference and being connected in a holistic way.

CHRIS

Why build your own community when there are so many real estate events, seminars, and conferences? Because they are missing the conversations of those who feel socially pulled to make a difference. If you have a social issue embedded in your soul, these events don't usually have the peers and the space to discuss it. If you want to talk about social justice you may have to go to another community of people who don't understand you as a real estate agent, which has its own benefits. There is an opportunity to work with agents who understand the profession and want to use it as an agent of change. Why can't real estate be an industry of social change rather than sales?

AARON

Real estate can be used for social change based on the structure and mechanisms of how this industry works. The industry is designed for us to be in communication with people in a way that no other industry has access to. We just haven't been taking advantage of it.

CHRIS

I've seen individual agents find their voice and be a steward for more cooperation. Then the ripple of the groundswell happens.

With over 20 years in business, **Chris Angell** has seen the dysfunctional and damaged relationship people have with marketing. 98% of people are cynical of what they see online and as business owners we can feel this and so we don't share in fear that people will be cynical of us and our Important work. As heart-centered entrepreneurs, we must find a healthy and empowered place to share our message which is why Chris has built powerful programs designed to make marketing easy and authentic.

TO CONTACT CHRIS

- chris@mygroundswell.com
- https://www.themindfulceo.com/

CAMBRIA & ROBERT HENRY

CHRISTINE

Anybody can read a book on how to sell 20 more houses. We want to talk about how to live an empowered life and how to help people who work with you do the same. You want your life to fulfill your reason for existence. It's a different game than getting FSBO scripts. Tell us why you got into real estate.

ROBERT

People shouldn't get into real estate unless they have a passion to help buyers and sellers. They should have passion for their client to not work with anyone else because they are going to go to the nth degree to get their client what he wants. If they don't have that drive, if they don't have that passion, they're going to be part of the statistic. They're going to be part of the percentage, which is nearly 90% now, who are out of the business within just a few years. If they want to start their own team, they must be fanatical about helping people grow and teaching them the skills that will make them successful in real estate.

Cambria and I got into real estate and started a team, and a brokerage because we wanted to fulfill that passion. We wanted to create and be part of an organization that was a catalyst for people coming on board and transforming their lives because they are part of our organization. If people don't have that kind of drive or that kind of passion, the real estate industry will chew you up and spit you out.

AARON

I was just looking at the people on our team, and I can see when there is passion to be part of the contribution. It shows up.

When you're talking about bringing agents on and into Haven as a brokerage, what's the interview process like and do you decline agents?

CAMBRIA

I interview about 30 people a month and we'll take on two, maybe three of them.

CHRISTINE

Do you have a team inside your brokerage? When you interview them, could they either be on your team or in your brokerage? Where do you find 30 people a month to interview?

ROBERT

They could end up on our team or on the brokerage and we do a couple of things that bring in that many people a month. We have an intense branding campaign. We have about 36 radio commercials that play a day and they feature some of our top agents. We had seven of our top performing agents shoot a commercial that says, "Hi, I'm Hannah Masters with Haven Real Estate Group. In the last year, I've had the privilege and opportunity to help over 30 families find their home. I'm so grateful that I chose a brokerage that provides the support, training and tools that lead me to being not only successful, but me being able to pursue my passion, which is helping people."

Then I jump in and say, "Look, if you're a real estate agent or you're considering being a real estate agent, and you feel like this kind of training and support would be beneficial to you, give us a call." We get about four to five inquiries a week from that. Then we have videos where our agents talk about the tools, training, and support they receive. It's a consistent drip.

AARON
Do those people come into the brokerage, and then you pick from those people who to join your team?

CAMBRIA
Yes. The first step is coming to our Tuesday training session. That way they get an idea of what they can expect week after week from us. If they don't like the first meeting, there's no reason to even move forward. We do look at mindset and we start each meeting asking our agents what they are grateful for. Then we talk about our personal development. We talk about how this job is not about sales. This job is about being an advocate. If you think real estate is about sales, our organization isn't right for you. We don't sit down and talk to people until after they've attended a Tuesday training session. We have had people come to meetings, leave, and never come back.

ROBERT
It took us a while to learn we had to instill that process. When

we had 15 agents in our brokerage, we were racing trying to get to 50. When we got to about 35 agents, we realized, because we focused on numbers, we had a lot of drama to clean up. We just had an unbelievable amount of weeding out to do as well as problems and challenges. We took a step back and we realized, we wanted people who have a passion and desire to grow in their lives. The correlation of their growth is going to have a direct and proportionate correlation to how much they serve others. When we were working at Landmark, 25% of the candidate in the room register. We apply many of the techniques that we learned there here.

AARON

Tell me about the difference between the brokerage and the team and how that works given it's your brokerage and your team.

CAMBRIA

The biggest difference is the number of leads and support they're given. They have a mentor on their team and the mentor is on top. If someone is experienced with a large sphere and they have a lot of repeat clients, they want our training, motivation, atmosphere, and culture that we have here, but they don't need as much support or hand holding. Those are the people who are on the brokerage side.

AARON

What is the split on the team?

ROBERT

The split on the team is 50/50. If they're an individual or solo agent, the split is 90/10 with a 200,000 cap. Training our agents early on to close one hundred transactions is how we have been successful. If you can close one hundred transactions that sets the longevity and sustainability of your career. The average happy client is going to refer an additional four pieces of business. Two things make our team successful. First, we realized the value of a single transaction is not that transaction. The value of a single transaction on average is four to five. We started doing our own marketing with respect to the lifetime value of a client to the firm. We focused on the percentage we were willing to spend up front to secure that client. We focus delivering to the client and then take market share.

It's interesting when agents that transition from the 50/50 model to the independent model because they hear us talk about our cost of acquisition for that first client. Often the firm loses money, but our focus has always been the long game. When the agent makes the transition to being independent if they skip any steps, they don't have a hundred past clients. They don't have that sphere. They don't have a marketing platform in place. They don't realize how much more work they must do when they become independent. Then they realize we weren't kidding when we say the firm takes a loss on that first transaction.

AARON

Agents rarely understand the expenses unless they've been educated to understand them.

When you bring people in, what's the agreement that make for their training on the team versus the brokerage? What other trainings and things do you offer to your team?

CAMBRIA

We do a Tuesday training. That's for everybody. We do a Wednesday training in our Spokane office. Then we repeat that same training in our Coolin office. If it has anything to do with legal forms, then we tailor it for the Idaho market versus the Washington market. Then we usually do a six-week mastery course. All of those are available to anybody, but they're more tailored to people on the team. It's not like somebody on our brokerage couldn't go to something if they wanted to. On top of that in the team, until you've done at least five transactions or your first 90 days, you have a mentor, and you stay inside a mentor group. That makes a big difference as well.

CHRISTINE

We have mentors. Do you do one on one mentoring? Tell me about your mentor group. Does one lead agent mentor them? Does that lead agent get an override on anything that they produce?

CAMBRIA

Usually, two to four agents will be inside the mentor group. We do extra training, but they do have more lead opportunities just for mentors. I'm about to send out a mail out to 15,000 people. The number on it will be for our mentor line. Only they have access to that phone number.

ROBERT

We have seven mentors and then we do one on one coaching with our mentors. To be a mentor they must have 20 or more transactions completed in the previous year. They must have recommendations from both staff and their peers. We presented and pitched the mentor role as a way for the mentors to get additional training as well. Typically, an agent will hit a plateau within their own production. We've showcased that the catalyst to taking your production to the next level is by contributing to your peers. After completing several six-month sessions, on average, they increase their productivity by 220%. After going to several sessions our agents can see how beneficial the sessions are.

CAMBRIA

People can start teams inside of Haven if they want to. Many of our mentors are interested in eventually breaking off, becoming independent, and starting their own team. We want to support them in that. Part of being a mentor is learning how to do that.

ROBERT

Everyone aspires to leadership. There's a very distinct difference between being a productive individual to managing others to leading. You use very different skill sets. Many of them will think because they're a high producer, they can rely on those skills to move into running a small group or team. About 60% to 70% of the mentors realize, after completing a six-month session, that having a team and being a mentor is a lot of work. Some are unsure if they want to switch to their own team because it's so daunting. That benefits us as well, because they realize while they can mentor an agent or two, there are a lot of complexities involved with moving and inspiring whole teams.

AARON

The Peter Principle states that everyone rises to their own level of incompetence. It was meant to be an inside joke when Lawrence Peters wrote it. Lawrence Peters is a Canadian economist and professor, who wrote the Peter Principle. In examining it, he discovered there's a culture in business that shows if you can do it, you can lead it. Therefore, people can have the skills, get into leadership, and find themselves to be incompetent, but that was the natural next step of the progression.

They turn out to be incompetent at the skill they need for leadership. Then, they can self-select themselves back down a level. It's a brilliant model for leaders to give people a chance to see if they can do something or if it's a skillset they are interested in acquiring. That's why we have that model in American business, because people assume I should be the next leader. That would be the natural path. I need someplace to expand. Letting them go up, fail, prove to themselves, and then come back on their own is great.

ROBERT
While we were building out our second brokerage, the owner of the brokerage we left, stopped by. He told us he was flabbergasted to see we were expanding into another state. They had bet against us. 95% of agents when they start a brokerage say it's because they want to retain one hundred percent of their commissions. They don't want to answer to anybody else. That drove us out and compelled us to double down on what we were doing.

We are in real estate, but that's not really the business we are in. We're in the human development and personal development business. We invest in people, and we work on elevating their skills. In addition to elevating their skills, we elevate what they believe within themselves is possible. That's the business we're in. That's what we focus on. It's so exhilarating because of its challenges. People will fight you every step of the way. That's just the human condition.

I remember when Aaron told me that I was spending more time internally and externally complaining about the very thing I had committed to doing than it would take to do complete the task. My initial response was to tell him he was wrong, but after thinking about it for a minute I realized he was right. The moment I started to focus on shortening that time, was when everything clicked for me. Every day we have things we are committed to accomplishing, but it's important to reconnect with that passion and why we are in real estate. The difference we want to make is what drives us. We had a single mow who was working for another company. At that company she closed three transactions over the course of two years and was thinking about quitting. After switching brokerages and working with us for six months, she closed 12 transactions. Afterwards, she walked into my office and told me she was able to enroll both of her children in private school and that before she worked with us, she never would have thought that was possible.

Last year we met with the CFO of Realogy. Realogy has seven different brands including Century 21 and Coldwell Banker. Because of that, he has access to the varying models between their hundreds or thousands of offices. After that conversation, I realized that models for teams and brokerages are all similar. Then we looked at the tools that were available. When we were looking into starting a brokerage, we interviewed all the major models, and we discovered there wasn't anything that made one more spectacular than the other. Some had better marketing materials, and some had better in-house training programs. Some had a better split. We realized that while everyone is trying to reinvent the wheel, they were missing the intention of developing leaders within the organization. That was what was missing. There are many franchises and organizations that tout training, but that training is designed to capture more buyers and sellers.

Most of them are teaching outdated models because building funnels, retargeting, remarketing, and making videos is hard to do. They're regurgitating the same information from our industry from the last 30 years. The side effect of focusing on elevating people's lives, elevating them to what feels possible, and shifting their mindset from one of survival to one of creating a life that really works for them, is they're much more enthusiastic about their career. They're more enthusiastic, grateful, and gracious with their clients. By focusing on them and their development they begin to perform at a higher level with a greater degree of satisfaction in their career.

On the other side, by focusing on agents developing themselves, we build a phenomenal culture. And then the other side effect of that is it builds a phenomenal culture. Most real estate offices are cold, quiet, and sterile. In our office everyone works together. They are giving each other hugs and high fives. There's greater energy, affection, and collaboration amongst our agents because they grow together.

AARON
We're not in the real estate business, we're in the people business. You must be fanatical about empowering people,

otherwise there is no point. You must hire people who are fanatical about helping people buy or sell their homes. Otherwise, it's another job and it's going to be brutal. Those people self-select themselves out of the business. The people who aren't aligned that way fail out because they came in wanting to be their own boss to schedule their own hours.

CAMBRIA

You schedule your own 90 hours.

ROBERT

My business coach often uses the phrase, "There's so much opportunity in the real estate business in terms of growing teams or growing a brokerage because the majority of brokerage owners and team owners are mailing it in." I finally asked him, "What do you mean by mailing it in?" He told me that we've ridden an economy that's done well in the last 12 or 13 years. He says when the high tide recedes, we're going to see a lot of people are out in the water playing a big game, but they don't have any pants on.

Leading a brokerage or a team can be challenging. It's tough. People have different personalities. Their levels of resistance are different. Their backgrounds and their filters are different. You really must tailor everything to the individual. There are not a lot of broker owners or team owners who are willing to go that deep. There are not a lot of team owners, brokerage owners who are willing to do the work, grow themselves, and get the coaching and training they need to make a difference for the people that they're serving.

Cambria and Robert Henry are the co-owners of Haven Real Estate Group, which they founded in 2015.

Cambria Henry is consistently ranked one of the top 10 Realtors® in Spokane, and is also one of the top-rated real estate agents in the country. She works with Haven's new agent training program, providing daily training and coaching. Before becoming a Realtor®, Cambria worked in construction management, founded a recruiting firm, and served as a leadership coach for a worldwide personal development company.

Robert Henry began his career as a Realtor® after working as a builder and general contractor. He works with more experienced agents, helping them to grow their business and develop leadership skills while maintaining a work-life balance.

He is a national public speaker on personal development, real estate training, and other topics.

TO CONTACT CAMBRIA & ROBERT

✉ cambria@havenrealestategroup.com
   robert@havenrealestategroup.com

🔗 https://havenrealestategroup.com/

/SpokaneHaven/

@havenrealestategroup

JEFF WILLMORE

AARON

Tell us about who you are and how we met.

JEFF

I met Aaron and Christine through many years of collaboration and partnership at Landmark Worldwide. It was an incredible privilege to lead those programs. Prior to that, I was an entrepreneur and in the business world. When I was I business for myself, I was only moderately successful and I realized if I didn't work my ass off, I wouldn't make it. Anyone who found a level of success worked hard to get there. If they weren't there yet, they weren't working hard enough. Throwing myself into work wasn't a problem for me because I was single and young. I was making money for the first time in my life, and it was fun.

I dedicated myself to getting better at business. I grew up in an entrepreneurial family and I liked being my own boss. Risking things was in my blood but I didn't know anything about business. So, I started taking courses and reading books. I forced myself to get a subscription to The Wall Street Journal and started to read that every day. I was also reading Business Week, Inc. Magazine, and Fast Company. Then one day I had the epiphany that everything I was learning and studying is what I now consider to be common knowledge.

I don't mean common in a pejorative way. I mean it's common, it's plentiful, and it's everywhere. There are things everyone knows, even if they aren't using those things. The moment I realized this, I realized everyone else was doing the same thing, or some version of it. This studying and learning was only making me more like everyone else and vice versa. There we were, in our market, competing with one another and fighting with one another using the same common knowledge that has made us all so similar. It didn't make sense. At the time I didn't mind working 70-hours a week. It was fun, but I could start to feel the grind and I realized this might not work out for me because I wasn't sure if I has headed in the direction I wanted to go.

I constantly felt like I wasn't being paid what I was worth. Competing on price is everywhere because you're competing with everyone else. If someone comes to you and teaches you how to do digital media, you may lean some useful things, but they are going next door to your competitors and teaching the same thing. Everyone is using the same common knowledge. I wanted to know where I could go that would give me access to fulfill my vision for my business. I didn't know what it was, I just felt that I had one.

I could feel it, but I couldn't articulate it. Many people who started their own company will say they did it because they wanted to be their own boss, but that's not why they started. We can't say why we started because it was just something we felt we had to do. We can't articulate what that feeling was. I wanted to access being true to my vision, and I couldn't find a way to articulate my vision anywhere. I considered getting my MBA and then decided against it because I would just be learning more common knowledge. That period in my life led me to Landmark. I walked into the forum and started doing different things to challenge my mindset and thinking. So, my brother and I sold our business because after returning from the forum that's what I wanted to do. That's where I met the two of you.

Forums have entire collections of people, and a handful of those people were incredibly successful, drive, and ambitious in their field. It made me realize that those people were making the same sacrifices I made. They're working as hard as they can. I remember thinking, "Someone has to create something that gives people a way out so they can both fulfill their ambitions and generate wealth, while not sacrificing their important commitments." My autonomy course was a dream that took 15 years to fulfill. When I launce the first one, I wasn't even sure if anyone would show up.

CHRISTINE

When did you launch the first one? How many people were on the first one?

JEFF

I launched the first course in 2018 and I just launched my fourth one. I remember when I first started, I told my wife that if at least 20 people showed up, it would be a go, but if only one person showed up then I would go on to do something else. Then, over 50 people showed up and I knew that this was something people wanted but they didn't know they wanted it because it hadn't been available before. If you consider yourself to be an entrepreneur, a business owner, or a leader, when someone is on your team, their productivity and success is a direct reflection of your function as leader and a business owner. People become who they are on your team because of the environment you create for your team. Unless that environment is consciously and intentionally created, you can end up with people who don't care about the team.

AARON
What steps can a team leader take to see their existing environment and alter it? How do they stay consistent when empowering people to fulfill their vision while fulfilling their own vision?

JEFF
My mindset is both the potential and the choke hold of our team. It's not about them. It's about my mindset. It takes real commitment on the part of a leader to look at themselves first.

CHRISTINE
Your course goes against everything people think they know about being successful. When you told me to slow down, I immediately thought you were crazy, but I understand the lesson now. I'm still telling my agents they need to work 70-hour weeks to make it a year after taking your course.

JEFF
The capacity to work hard is a necessary skill. It should be there to use when you need to use it. If you examine productivity and success, you see that the things that are promoted in the world come from a combination of motivation and hard work. If I stay motivated, work hard, and copy what

other people have done to become successful, I'm going to end up where I want to be. The problem is, for everyone who did all those things, I can show you a million people those things didn't work for. There are people who aren't successful even though they showed up to work every day, worked hard, had a good attitude, and did everything they were supposed to do. To stand out and be successful you must make yourself distinct.

CHRISTINE
It's brilliant when you say we need to offer something distinct. What makes you distinct from the other agents?

JEFF
If someone asks the two of you why they should hire you, your answer is going to be better than most because you're in the top 5%, but the reason will sound a lot like the others who are also in the 5%.

CHRISTINE
The agents who are nowhere near us can't compete, but I'm competing with the other ones, and we're all saying and doing the same thing.

JEFF
The more you compete in that way with the same language, which is through motivation and hard work, the more draining it becomes.

CHRISTINE
We're very distinct. We do communication and integrity. Tell us a little bit about your coaching offers.

AARON

There are tried and true things that work in real estate, like working 70 hours a week, making the contacts, and dialing the calls. These things aren't required but they are sufficient. The ability to work hard and keep the right mindset is required, but not sufficient to guarantee success. Keeping your goals is required but not sufficient. What ingredient needs to be added to make it sufficient?

JEFF

People must start with the basics, and they must be committed to being an expert in their field. Assuming someone's developed their expertise in their field, I propose that someone's ability and capacity to see the market uniquely and differently gives them a competitive advantage no one can copy, mimic, or take from them. It's priceless. It will give them different choices. It will give them different conversations. It will have them speaking differently.

When they are in meetings with clients or potential clients, they'll hear things no one else hears. They'll speak to concerns and commitment that you would normally miss. If a professional is committed and they're willing to educate their mind to engage with the marketplace differently, so they see it differently and asset it differently, it gives them a unique competitive advantage. Then they can step out of the world of working 70 hours a week to make it. It's not about being strategic with a niche to capitalize on it. It's not about doing things for the notoriety. It's about doing things because you feel as though you must do them.

AARON

Then your offering becomes finding a way to communicate that to the market. How do you communicate your worth as a realtor, as an agent, or as a team leader, if you're out recruiting people to be on your team?

JEFF

It's challenging because I can't just tell people what I did and then have them copy that. You two have developed and work on your own unique design and creation, which takes real thinking. It's not going to happen overnight. If it did it would be too superficial. One of the unique challenges that is the case for almost any business is connecting to what you want your life to be about. Reaching your goals takes real thinking. It requires designing and creating your business to be something more than just business. My real estate business, for example, allows me to fulfill the purpose of my life.

AARON

I hadn't articulated my life purpose. It had been washed up in the world of business. My career was a good way to make money and gave me some free time to spend with my family. It gives me enough of a financial cushion that I don't have to be freaked out about the future.

CHRISTINE

How can real estate fulfill my mission in life?

JEFF

Another example of common knowledge in the business world is to do what you love, and the money will follow. That's terrible advice. I can't sit just sit on a beach in Hawaii to bring in money. I'm not saying people shouldn't do what they love and shouldn't be connected to their offer, but the marketplace doesn't care about us. It doesn't care what we're committed to. It doesn't care if we have good hearts or not. The marketplace will be fine if you fail and go bankrupt. That's how the marketplace functions.

People in the real estate world should know who they are is what they are offering. Few people have been given the opportunity or the methodology to design their offer. They're left with the knowledge they've inherited which is usually some form of working hard and taking care of their customers at a fair price. They say they'll answer calls 24/7. If a client calls them on Saturday night about a house they saw on Zillow, they'll set up a showing on Sunday and be there for their client.

CHRISTINE
Mine offer is, "I'll get you more money than anybody else with less time," but who doesn't say that?

JEFF
That's an important part of your offer, but it's not the priceless part. That's not the part that connects with someone's heart and soul that makes the offer invaluable. The offers that connect with people's hearts are the compelling ones.

AARON
It's great for agents to think about what in their offer rises above price. What is it like working with me that no one else does or claims to do? It's a great question to develop instead of trying to force a marketing slogan.

JEFF

Agents must know the important commitments their clients have. Their offer must speak to the person they're interacting with. It should speak to that person and fulfill something that client is looking for. It might have nothing to do with buying or selling a house. They might not even be thinking about it. For example, Harley-Davidson doesn't sell motorcycles, you can buy a better bike for less money. They sell people on doing freedom rides. I have a Harley-Davidson, and I go to the freedom rides. I have a group I meet up with and we ride together on the weekends. Harley-Davidson offers me these parts of my life that are invaluable.

AARON

Even if someone doesn't go on those rides, they can see that vision, because it has been created. When people work with Christine and me, we offer them a life time working relationship. There is never a time when our client won't have a friend in real estate. There is no point where they don't have someone they can go to with questions about housing, plumbing, or whatever. That's not radically unique, though. That's common in this field. There is a family aspect we provide that is unique and has the flavor of what we're talking about.

CHRISTINE

I'm sure people can live a magical life in real estate, but that is not the foundation I work from.

JEFF

It's the common knowledge that ends up being the bad advice. Then people think they need to switch careers because the feel disconnected from their vision. That's why it takes real thinking. Just because it hasn't been created doesn't mean it can't be created. If it's all based on the circumstances, before you know it, we'll all be on the beach in Hawaii waiting for money to come in.

AARON

Is there a book that influenced your life that you would recommend for other people?

JEFF

I'm reading Dare to Lead by Brené Brown. One of the things that struck me while I was reading the book was how much entrepreneurs and professionals dress rehearse for tragedy to prepare ourselves for failure. Because of that, we don't experience joy. We don't let ourselves experience joy daily. She researched what makes someone more likely to experience joy because that's the most vulnerable experience we have and what's on the other side of it is tragedy. She discovered people who practice gratitude have the most joy in their lives.

**Jeff Willmore** has led transformational programs for over 23 years to over 160,000 people all over the world. He has worked with Olympic and professional athletes, Navy Seal and Special Forces members, top executives from all fields, Oscar winning actors, Grammy Award winning musicians— He's trained with the best and worked with the best! Jeff owes much of his development, abilities, and skills to the extensive training and development he got in transformational methodologies at Landmark Worldwide— very likely the top, personal transformational coaching faculty in the world.

Jeff has worked on the principles behind The Autonomy Course for over 10 years. He designed the Course using the latest research in cognitive science (How do we know what we know? How do we learn?), behavioral economics, ontology, and biology. The unique structure and methodology deliberately steps away from the "tips and techniques" kind of business knowledge that betrays top performance and living true and, instead, allows you to embody the advanced knowledge of a market leader and design leading-edge practices based on your own original thinking.

TO CONTACT JEFF

- ✉ jeff@jeffwillmore.org
- 🔗 https://autonomycourse.com/
- f /jeffwillmore.org
- @ @jeff_willmore
- ▶ @jeffwillmore789
- in /in/jwillmore/

JESSE ZAGORSKY

CHRISTINE

All right, well, Jesse, so just to get started, first of all, we've been looking forward to this for months. Just because you're one of the favorite people we have to talk to.

AARON

Thanks for being here. And then just so that people know who you are, get some history, give us some background. Jesse Zagorsky. eXp maven. Who are you?

JESSE

Yeah, I've been in real estate for 18 years, and I jokingly say I've done every single job in a real estate office. I have been a listing agent, a buyer's agent. I've answered phones and booked appointments for other people. I've been a team leader. I've cleaned toilets. I've been the broker of record. You name it, I've probably done it in an office. And I've been business partners with my mom for my entire career. So I'm a mama's boy. It's awesome for that. And I love running teams, I love supporting agents, and I'm also a systems guy.

That's kind of me in a nutshell.

CHRISTINE

Great. That's excellent. And you're out of San Diego.

JESSE

Out of San Diego, California. My last team I ran was about 21 agents. I shrank it, shrank it, shrank it until I dissolved it actually about a month and a half ago. So I still do my own deals, but I have some loose agents on the team. But I basically shut down my actual team so I could support more of the organization that I run within eXp. But also I realized I wasn't cut out to be a team leader. Maybe that's something we want to talk about today.

AARON

Yeah, that would be great.

JESSE

Now, Christine is a fantastic team leader. Aaron, you're an incredible leader. There's a big difference between being a team leader and a leader. I think I'm a good leader. I was a terrible team leader for real estate business, but we could unpack that if it's useful.

CHRISTINE

Well, that's a good let's tell us what's the difference?

JESSE

So I'm curious if you agree, Christine, because I believe that my biggest downfall as a team leader was I was too nice. I was too nice and I was a bit of an enabler. What I mean by that is I've run teams for 15 years of my career and I've had good teams and bad teams, high performance where they sold a little, sold a lot. I've screwed it up a lot of times. And the biggest times I've screwed it up is when I've had large teams where I didn't protect the culture of the team as it was growing and I let anyone join and I didn't fire people because I'm too nice, right. I didn't let them go. And so my culture would kind of erode from being this top producer culture down to, like, medium producer, and then your top producers get really frustrated and they quit. Your lowest producers who should have been fired, they eventually get frustrated and leave anyway, and you're left with this kind of middle of the road that sells a few houses. Maybe they don't. And I really think that most of the team leaders I know are incredible with boundaries, incredible with setting out. Like, here's the mission. You're either on the bus or you're off. And they're like, get the heck out of my team. I see that a lot in team leaders. Do you agree with that assessment, Christine, or do you run yours differently?

CHRISTINE

No, I think that Aaron does accuse me of keeping people too long, but I am my culture. If you're not on we launched that 90 day challenge the other day. I told you about Jesse, and there were three people that popped on three minutes late. They didn't get in. I don't mess around with that. Right. So I am like, you do what you say. It's not okay to fail. But I am somebody who unfortunately, is very hopeful that at any moment this person's going to have a breakthrough.

JESSE

Yes.

CHRISTINE

And they end up costing me everything. So you're right on.

JESSE

Yeah.

AARON

When Christine says "I love that person" then they have an infinite runway.

JESSE

It's not serving Christine and it's not serving them.

AARON

Totally. It absolutely does not.

CHRISTINE

I think the struggle is, like, I have a girl right now who I think still to this minute is going to be spectacular. But she's been with us for five months and done zero.

JESSE

Okay. So can we flip that script? So let's give an actionable tip to the reader. I like actionable things. Write this down. Yeah. I don't know who taught me this, but it's incredibly true. And I think this might help you, Christine, if you don't already know it. Yes. At some point, this agent has been there five months, may have a breakthrough. She may. I'm not saying she will or won't. She might be an incredible human being, but the only way you can support an agent like that is in a group setting because any time that you dedicate to that person is taking time away from a top producer who could really use your help. And the most important resource we have is time as team leaders, as human beings, time. Right. And so what I want you to write down is most leaders spend the majority of their time helping the lowest 20%.

Instead, if you flip it, as leaders, we want to spend the majority of our time helping the top 20%. Double down on your leaders. See if you can get them to scale and grow. Pour into them and let everyone else swim for themselves. Don't ignore them, train them in the group, but the ones who rise up, then you pour into them. Does that make sense?

CHRISTINE

You're 100% bang on. Like we have a productivity coach that coaches everybody. Now, once you're at tier three, I'll coach you.

JESSE

Right.

CHRISTINE

But we're with our team every morning, as you know, on a huddle call at 08:00 a.m. Where everybody gets to be a part of it and it's a very big piece of our culture. If you missed a huddle call a couple of times, you're going to probably not be on our team for very long.

AARON

Well, integrity is one of those lines that really is super critical for our culture. But that thing you just said, I would say it the way I've been taught it from my leading at Landmark in general is you lead to the top. When you're leading, you lead to the top and everyone else rises up because if you don't, you suppress the top down because they know how you get attention is to fail.

JESSE

I've never heard that, but I love that, Aaron, and that was what I was going to say. I was going to put it back to you because, Aaron, you are such a great natural complement to Christine because your leadership style is similar, but you occur differently in the world for people. Yeah. You guys balance each other out really.

AARON

Well everybody thinks we're an old married couple because we bicker.

CHRISTINE

We do not. And then they get with our productivity coaches about being nice. It really doesn't serve people. The one thing I think is I'd love to hear your take on it, given your history with so many different teams, but our view is pretty much if you do certain work, it's going to produce the results. So if you talk to 20 people a day about real estate, you're going to produce the results. We don't really have to guess about that.

AARON

It doesn't matter how you talk to them. Facebook, social media, whatever, right. Maybe we got to tweak your scripts.

But you press in and you talk to 20 human beings a day.

JESSE

May I push back on that slightly? I agree. But I also disagree. So I've been saying something a lot lately that I don't know where I got it from, but I'm going to loop it in here. I've been saying the way you feel is more important than what you do. The way you feel is more important than what you do.

AARON

We got to talk about this.

JESSE

I know, and I used to be the opposite. That's why I think it's interesting to discuss, because here's what I think. If you talk to 20 people a day, if I went out there to totally try to self sabotage and I was the worst salesperson on the planet, I could literally talk to 20 people a day and still fail. It's not the action, but most salespeople, when you give them a concrete micro commitment, because talking to 20 people a day, it is a challenging thing, but it's still very concrete, and it's a stretch for people. So who they become in doing that 20 per people a day actually changes who they are being, and it's the way they're engaging with those people because real estate is a contact sport. 100%. You talk to enough people, you're going to get some success.

But I had 21 agents on my team in January of 2019. Guess how many houses they sold in January of 2019? 21 people.

CHRISTINE

No!

JESSE

I got a full shutout in January of 2019. We sold zero houses. Okay. I lost $40,000 as a team leader in February of 2019, I lost $25,000. We sold a few houses, still lost money as a team. That's when I started realizing that I kept doing this law of large numbers because they were doing the actions, some of them like, crappy actions. If they would have talked to 20 a day, we probably would have sold some houses. But who they were being in the moment were broken. I'm being very dramatic, but broken shells of human beings. Truly, like, the culture in our team was like, I got to do this stuff that sucks that Jesse says to do.

AARON

Okay, sorry I'm interrupted. Okay, good. But here's what I would jump in with.

So I definitely get what you're saying, and I think you're right. Okay? I don't think you're wrong. I do think you're right. The context in which you operate absolutely is going to make a difference in your action.

CHRISTINE

Jesse, I did this on your two minute thing. Teach long something, right? The context is decisive. If you get on lead gen and you're like, this sucks. I suck at this. Life sucks. You're dead. You're dust. It doesn't matter what you do.

JESSE

Good.

AARON

But here's the other piece, okay? Here's the other side of it. I think, Jesse, I think you will definitely agree with this until you're doing the 20 conversations, until you're taking the actions, I don't care what your mindset is. Nothing's going to happen. The mindset is not going to produce how you feel is not going to produce the result.

JESSE

Correct.

CHRISTINE

They have to go together.

AARON

I take the actions, and then I can coach your mindset, but I can't coach your mindset until you're taking the actions.

JESSE

Yes, it starts with action. It always starts with action. And also, though I will give credit to Tony Robbins on this one, Tony Robbins talks about giving yourself the results before you get the results through visualization. Totally. So, how do you get someone to take action? There's only certain human beings that when Aaron and Christine say, go talk to 20 people a day, they're going to say, that sounds great, I'm totally going to do that tomorrow.

And they're going to say, I'm going to do that tomorrow for like, six months till they fail off the team, right? Oh, it's already new. And I haven't talked to many people. I'm done with it for today. That's what normal human beings do. But when you can give them a taste or an experience of the results before they actually start doing it, visualize yourself talking to 20 people. Visualize yourself. Get that perception. So I do think you, in a way, are coaching the mindset a little bit totally.

To get them into action. Get them into action. And then you can go and refine the mindset even more.

CHRISTINE

Like, our 90 day challenge that we did the other day is so much fun. And we did it live, and it was 4 hours or 5 hours, and we dealt with a lot of that. The hardest part was getting them to say what they wanted to do with the money. Once they got the money, we're like, okay, if you do this many houses, you're going to end up with 90 grand in your pocket. What are you going to do? And they're like, I'd be like, to get them to think outside, think outside that box.

And then we're like, and what are you willing to put at stake at that for that? It was like crickets. Because they do have the capacity. They don't have that mastery of mind. Awesome. All right, well, the three of us can't not I mean, look, we're 23 minutes in and we haven't talked about how we all are interacting and how we are connected. I know Jesse and I met at a company I will not mention. So for those of you reading, Jesse is the reason that Aaron and I are at eXp, which was the best move we've ever made.

AARON

Super excited about it. We're like, literally holding on to his coattails and saying, let's go. So, I mean, you've done some extraordinary, extraordinary things in the three years you've been with eXp or just over two years, something like that. Can you share a little bit about that? With everybody who's watching.

JESSE

Yeah. The funny thing is, you weren't excited about eXp at the beginning. You came kicking and screaming.

CHRISTINE

Do you remember me walking into that lunch? I was like, I'm not changing brokerages.

JESSE

Yeah, you sat down and you bled red, and you're like, I ain't coming ever. Right? Not going to name your formal company. It's a fantastic company. But you're like, I am never leaving. Please don't even talk to me about this. But, fine, you want to talk to me. And then once you saw I think you saw what I saw, which was, to me, my favorite part is the collaboration. And it's incentivized leadership that eXp creates. It's not the company, it's not the model.

It's the connection of human beings, because this podcast is all about empowerment. It creates empowerment in a way that you and I could have never been business partners. I live in San Diego. You live in Seattle. We both run big teams. Aaron's doing his thing. There would be no way in any meaningful light that we could actually be connected. eXp allows us to share and align our financial interests, and now we just get to support and pour into agents. So, in my own brokerage, I had 41 agents at my independent company. I'd run it for 14 years. We weren't ever trying to be the biggest, the baddest.

We wanted to be a small group of really high level individuals. And there's a lot of indie brokerages out there like that. So fast forward three years later in eXp. I've brought over 36 people to eXp in 36 months. I'm going just on three years. So three years is 36 months. 36 agents. Some people listening might be like, wow, you recruited 36 people? That's terrible.

It's one a month. If any broker owners are listening, just think in your head. You hire a recruiter and they bring you one new agent a month. You would fire them in a month or two months, right? They'd be done. And so I brought over 36 people. Those 36 have allowed me to shift some of my transaction based income for referral based income, because I referred 36 to the company. They referred other people, referred their friends.

I now have a group that I look at it like, I own a brokerage, only legally. It's not a brokerage. I own a brokerage of 731 agents. I don't know all 731. I don't talk to all of them. I talk to the ones who are swimming towards me, right? I pour into the ones that we align, but the other ones, when they sell a house, I still get paid part of the commission that comes out of eXp side. So I'm making 40 grand a month in residual income.

CHRISTINE

After three years in this company with no expenses and no liability, we're not even talking about stock yet, right?

JESSE

Yeah. And I have over half a million dollars in stock, right, that I wouldn't have had. I'm talking fast now, so I probably won't get as emotional. But when I really stop and think about it, I have a three year old and a six year old. If I would have kept running the company that I was running, I literally have half a million dollars sitting in an account that I don't need that money right now. That money is for my kids.

It is sitting there for their college, for their life, whatever they want to do with it. I don't care. Right. But it's changed my family's destiny without a shout out of a doubt.

AARON

Awesome.

CHRISTINE

I remember sitting there with you, and I was 20 minutes into the lunch and I literally said, I'm going to this thing with Jesse. I just brought on a team leader who was a friend. I was on her dead to me list when I finally left, but we wanted to go.

JESSE

The financial upside is huge. The stock is huge. It saves most agents tons of money switching over. But to me, it really is the people. You're not joining a company. You join people. Like anyone listening to this podcast has seen the value of what you and Aaron do and what you guys bring. They would get to be business partners with you guys. That's my favorite part.

CHRISTINE

I knew you for years before I didn't talk to you this much. I talk whenever I need to now.

JESSE

It's just good human beings aligning. That's what I love about this.

AARON

Yeah, and that's the beauty of it, too, because you say it like that, like, it's just good people aligning. And at the same time, I'm not just taking random calls from people that don't pay me. There's a financial incentive to you know what I mean? Like, okay, I'm not out to be a jerk about it, but at the same time, I'm not just like, oh, here's all my you were just talking about before the call. Like, this person's three people down right in the organization, and you're like, but yeah, that's my people. I'm taking the time.

I don't take random coaching calls for free.

JESSE

No. Okay, so let me give a recruiting tip that they probably already know, but I learned this from a guy named John Cheplach, who is one of my recruiting coaches. Love Cheplac. He said the best way to recruit someone is to create the experience of what it's like for someone to be at your company or your team before they actually ever make the switch.

CHRISTINE

You told me that. That's awesome, right?

JESSE

I'm wired to be a naturally helpful human being. So are you, Christine. So are you, Aaron. It's rewarding people for being the human beings they've been. That's all it is. It's just finding a system to reward people for doing stuff they love doing. Yeah.

CHRISTINE

That is one of the things I find absolutely shocking, though. I mean, if you think about these two that you and I talked to the other day. I know them from Landmark, right? I led her seminar four or five years ago. And they hear about eXp and they hear about eXp, but people ever really they hear whatever they hear, they never really get it. They were ready to go to Compass. They were signed up, ready to go on Thursday leaving for Compass. But we thought we'd talk to you anyway, even though we know we're going to Compass. And, like, within a half hour, they're like, wow, this is all about empowerment.

I'm like, how do people not know.

AARON

That this is what this company is.

CHRISTINE

Empowering everybody to win. You know, it's amazing to me when people really get what it's just like me sitting there. When I really got it, I was all, Shit, I'm leaving my brokerage.

JESSE

Yeah, I was more colorful than you in my language. I don't even curse. But when I saw it, it took me about I said no for nine months. I didn't even look at it. When I actually sat down to look at it, it took about seven minutes and I dropped an F bomb.

I shut down my company. I was pissed.

JESSE

So this is where, by the way, I'll have to say, I wasted months and months on going down rabbit holes, because you can't spend all day trying to unlock every door. You can't. But I would in a LinkedIn conversation where it will take an extra six sentence, I would banter back one time, Aaron, if you want a little tip. And this is, by the way, anybody recruiting.

And this works, by the way. If you're listening to this and you're not. At eXp, this same technique works for everything. You have to pivot and get curious. That's the words. Remember? Pivot and get curious. So you got some immediate pushback at a high level. There's only two reasons why people won't do business with you. By do business, I mean be recruited by you, work with you as a buyer, as a seller. The only two reasons they feel threatened or they don't see the value.

They feel threatened or they don't see the value. Do you want me to unpack those or those make sense to you?

AARON

Those make sense.

JESSE

Okay, so in this case, where you're talking to someone on LinkedIn and he's a recruiter for another company, and he gives you a strong pushback. I am not recruitable. I am a recruiter. I've been pitched by eXp before. Hard pass. Not for me, thank you. Maybe even say thank you. What do you think it was? Is it he feels threatened, he doesn't see the value, or both? What do you think?

AARON

I think it's probably a little both that maybe doesn't see the value.

JESSE

100% both. 100% both. The reason you got such a strong response is because he feels threatened. An animal backed into a corner will show you its claws. Right? Gentleman is, probably very polite in general, but you got a very curt response. Maybe he's not. Who knows? But I'm guessing you got more of a curt response because he's like, I'm shutting this down right now. You are not going to trick me into doing something that I don't want to do. No, thank you.

That's what I mean by threatened. See, the value is, clearly whoever talked to him before didn't spend enough time to actually recruit him. My favorite definition of recruitment is spending the time to understand someone's hopes, dreams, and goals and then being the bridge to help them get there. So they came at him in the previous conversations with an eXp model without they prescribed before they diagnosis.

CHRISTINE

They had no idea what he wants. If he doesn't care about he doesn't care about recruiting. But he loves stock. I mean, they just didn't care about what they didn't know what he wanted.

JESSE

Correct. So now that you know that Aaron going back to the scenario where you get this response where he basically says, hey, I'm a recruiter, first of all, in your head, you should be thinking, dude, he's a recruiter. I want to recruit this guy. I'm all in. Right? We need to know if he's on a salary or not, because that's one of the hurdles to recruit someone, is what are the challenges in their life?

My affirmation is I'm a creative, creative, solution oriented problem solving machine. I'm a creative, solution oriented problem solving machine, as you said, over and over my head in my 20s. Anyway. So I'm looking for data points, looking for how do I solve this guy's challenge? But I'm going to come back to him in LinkedIn message. Very simply, I'm going to say, totally respect that. I would never want you to do something you don't want to do. I'm curious. What are you focused on? What are your goals?

And I wouldn't ask both questions. I'd pick one or the other. What lights you up? Something that open up, because people love talking about themselves and what they want to do. And then I'm going to go back and forth. I'm going to get him to tell me some things that are interesting until I find something that legitimately is interesting that he says. And then I'm going to say, wow, that's really cool. Let's jump on a quick phone call or zoom. I want to learn more. And then I'm going to get on voice to voice, and I'm going to go deeper, because most people don't bear their soul on LinkedIn text message DM.

You want to learn to master recruitment? I mean, you don't have to. You can only recruit other high DS if you want to just recruit one group of people you can alienate, which are great people to recruit. But if you want to alienate 90% of the world, by all means, don't. Learn or grow. I'm kidding.

This is where I've coached enough people who are high DS in recruitment that this is the hardest part for you.

AARON

I totally get it.

JESSE

Because when you talk to someone, normally you say, hey, you want to join our team? I want to join Christine and Co. Right. Recruitment is the opposite. I tell people I'm joining their team. Right? You want me to join your team. You couldn't afford to pay me as a coach. I'm not for sale. But when you join eXp, I work for you. You tell me what you need, you point the right direction. I'm joining your team.

As a D, you're like, that's just a weird thing to say, but I'm telling you, it melts people's hearts.

AARON

No, that's great. I totally get it. Absolutely. I need them, so that's perfect. And as a high D, I appreciate the coaching.

JESSE

Are you ready for this? This will stay at home. Do you have any friends from the south?

AARON

No.

JESSE

You'll never forget this now, because I've never thought about using the smiley face emoji like this. But you just blessed his heart. Do you know that expression?

AARON

I do know enough about that.

JESSE

So when someone's from the south and they're about to trash talk you and rip you apart, they say, real kind, Bless your heart. But you're a dirt bag. You can basically say anything after Bless your heart and get away with it because you just say, well, bless your heart. So by using the smiley face emoji, you didn't actually negate the combativeness. But I appreciate the idea.

AARON

Jesse, what books are you reading?

JESSE

I got a good one. Tell me if you guys have heard of this one. I am reading right now. I got to pull up the name of it. I am reading Jordan B. Peterson, Twelve Rules for Life.

AARON

I've heard of him.

JESSE

Professor from Canada. Gave a bunch of Ted Talks that went viral, wrote this book. Someone told me, don't buy the book. Just watch the Ted Talks. But I bought the book anyway because.

Live. Love. San Diego Homes is co-owned by **Jesse Zagorsky**, a licensed California Real Estate Broker. He has been active in San Diego Real Estate for 10+ years, and has sold over 500 homes. Jesse's passion for Real Estate includes helping his clients find the perfect home, helping investors analyze possible returns, and Sellers maximize their sales price through tested techniques. With a background in Marketing, Jesse loves creating a total marketing experience for each of ZTeam's listings.

TO CONTACT JESSE

- jesse@livelovesdhomes.com
- https://theagentcollective.com/contact-us/
- /in/jesse-zagorsky-5b13967

LISA MAYSONET

CHRISTINE

How do you empower your agents to be successful without your constant help? How big is your team or brokerage? Tell us about yourself.

LISA

I work for Sotheby's International Realty. I've been an agent there for over 40 years. I started when I was about 16. My boyfriend's mother, who is now my husband, was the head of a large real estate company in Manhattan. That was my first job. I Typed leases and did filing. I quickly got into sales, and I did onsite sales. I've sold every type of product, conversions, ground up, and new development projects. The only part of that business that isn't my forte is the paperwork, but I have support for that. It works out well.

CHRISTINE

Do you have a team?

LISA

I have a team in the city. About a year and a half ago, I expanded to the Hamptons and out on Long Island. I've been out here for 25 years. Now I'm representing properties as well as enjoying the Hamptons, which is incredible. It's a beautiful part of the world. There are incredible beaches and luxury in every area. It's very quaint, elegant, sophisticated, and charming.

My team is doing incredible in the city. We've done 50% more deals than during the height of the market, back in 2004. I closed on a $7.6 million deal we did over Zoom. He never saw it until after he closed. It's a different world now in many ways. It was a unique experience and maybe even a one-off lottery ticket experience, but I see it as all new possibilities. Things are being created now that never would have been thought of before. I start at growth. The world was pivoting. That was the buzz word. I was using possibilities and growth. I always wanted to expand and thought I would expand somewhere else. Here I am in the Hamptons, but I was in the city on Tuesday. A lot of Manhattan-ites come to the Hamptons. It's their summer playground.

So, I've been selling real estate or involved in real estate since I was 16. I love it. I couldn't think of doing anything else, other than being Barbra Walters, I would want to be. I get to see and represent incredible properties. It's my love, it's my passion. I am also passionate about my family. I come from a European background where everybody is about family, and we have extended family all over the world.

I do a lot of charitable work for the homeless youth because children are so vulnerable, and they have no one to protect them. I work with God's Love We Deliver, which is a charity that delivers food to people who can't feed themselves because they're too sick. So, my three passions are real estate, my family, and my charities. Even the charity work is real estate related. I don't like to think about children living on the street.

This is a very up and down business in every way. You have a deal, or you don't have a deal. Your emotions are high. Your emotions are low. Your energy is high. Every day is different, especially when you start growing and beginning to love sales or when you are wearing the managerial hat as well.

How do you make decisions, so you live an abundant life? There is a difference between a crystal ball and a rubber ball. It's a crystal ball if it's a decision you can never get back, like your only child graduating from law school, helping your child deliver their baby, or a $100 million project and you have a meeting with the developers. If it's a rubber ball, you can throw or bounce it to someone else. If it's a crystal ball it shatters, and you can't get it back.

On my team, we have two sayings that go around, that we use a lot. One of them is, "You can never go wrong by doing the right thing." When we have to make decisions, we must think about if it's right or ethical, especially when you're working with another agent. Sellers and buyers come and go, but you'll have to work with that agent again. It's important. Our second saying is, "Together each accomplishes more." We value that saying as well.

CHRISTINE
How big is your team?

LISA
I have a full-time marketing person and a full-time administrative assistant. I have three agents in the city and two and half out here because the marketing person is now getting her license. She'll be able to do some showings.

CHRISTINE

We love how expectations differ from each team leader. Some people have expectations that people on their team perform each month and other people don't have that expectation. Where do you fall on that spectrum? Do you expect each team member to perform each month, or do you let them go at their own pace?

LISA

What's the point of having a salesperson if they aren't producing? If that's their job, and they aren't doing their job, what's the point? I love to help my team members grow. I want to work with agents who want to do business, and who want to grow. I can help them fulfill their potential. I know many team leaders who want people on their team to use them for things they don't want to do. Maybe they feel the younger team member is better at social media, but that doesn't help the agents, that helps the team leader.

Going back to our saying, "Together each accomplishes more." For example, if my team were a car, I may be the motor, but my admin is the person steering the car. The salespeople are the wheels on the tires. If any one of those doesn't function properly the car's not going far. I think everybody has a purpose. I think everybody has to do their job. I want to work with somebody who wants to grow and reach a potential. Then, you must approach the retainer-ship situation. I've learned the hard way, when you lose a team member, they take the people you've introduced them to and start communicating with your clients. I don't let my team members handle business 100% on their own. I stay involved and am the direct contact.

CHRISTINE

Even if your agents are working on a deal with someone, you're still the point of contact?

LISA

If I'm providing the source of the business or the lead, then yes. If it's their own business, they are the point of contact, I'm there to support them. Many of them supplement a lot of their income from business I give them. It's a win-win situation because it's business I wanted to share and it's better to keep it in house and on the team. I've gotten unlucky with some and then I've gotten very lucky with others. I haven agents I've been with six and seven years and we're still very loyal to each other. You have to find the right people and the right personality mix. What's your experience with that?

CHRISTINE

We're dealing with it right now. Aaron's the reason I have a team. We've known each other for 20 years and eight years ago he came and said, "I'm joining your team." I said I didn't have one. Then he let me know that I had a team now. We've grown from four or five agents to 20 agents. We've expanded. We are reconciling with ourselves right now about what kind of team we want and if we what to keep that high expectation, which many people can't meet. We had an agent who was on our team for a week, she said she couldn't do all the things we wanted her to do.

LISA

There has to be a balance and you must know their personalities. When they come on your team you give them a 90 day. You are going to support someone who wants to grow and be supported. The rest are going to fall out anyway. That's okay because it's not worth it to give energy to someone who isn't going to make it in sales.

AARON

How much business do your agents generate on their own and how much business do you hand them?

LISA

With each agent it's going to be different. The agents who don't last on my team are the ones who are not bringing in their own business. The only reason to have a team member is if they add to your bottom line and you add to their bottom line. If that's not happening, it's bad. I don't even know what to do with them. I don't want them to resent me because I didn't make them a superstar, but I end up resenting them because they're not bringing in business.

AARON

That's exactly how it goes. When you say you hand them business, are those past clients you're giving them? Do you provide paper click leads? Do you have a CRM that fills with leads? How much of your business is generated that way? Is it all referral? Are they expected to get their own business based on what you provide them?

LISA

If it's a property I don't want to show in the city, I'll bring on an agent and I'll assign that listing to them and we'll work together. Then they'll get a little piece of the pie.

CHRISTINE

Do they get the unrepresented buyers who call on that property if that's their property?

LISA

Anything that comes because of that would have the same deal. It's just like if they brought in a listing. Any of those buyers would fall under their deal. Whatever I do for them, I do for me. It works the same way.

CHRISTINE

That's very much the way we do it as well. Although I believe in New York, you must go to every showing. We don't have to do that here. People can get in with their super box. If it's their listing, the agent gets all the sign calls. They get all the leads, and we'll do all the staging.

LISA

I always show my own properties. Because I don't think anybody can do a better job than me. I'll show the other agent around. I'll show the direct buyer around. I'll show my agents how to show it. I want to sell that property quickly. I want everything done perfectly. If I see an agent is not doing something, I'll even step in and get the job done. Whatever needs to be done. My bottom line is the same. Get that property sold.

CHRISTINE

If you were talking to somebody who is thinking of starting a team. What should they do if they want to empower and retain their team? What would be the number one tip you would give them?

LISA

It's important to have sales meetings because that keeps everybody on track. You're setting goals. You're connecting. I think that that's important.

AARON

How often do you do that?

LISA

I used to do it every week, but that was when we were meeting in person. When we stopped meeting in person, I was still doing it every other week. Once we shut down due to COVID for many months, we only held it once a month. Now, we are very busy. It's an important thing to do. I try to see everyone and talk to them at least once a week. Now that everybody is spread all over, I share a lot of information. I ask if they need support in any areas and give them a lot of feedback. As we are starting to open more, I'm going to turn up the heat. It's been on simmer for 16 months. We have to get more disciplined and focused again. You can retain the snow day a couple of different ways and still be on track.

What kind of goals do you have?

CHRISTINE

I'm committed to building passive income for my agents, so they don't ever have to worry about that.

LISA

How do you go about doing that?

CHRISTINE

We're with the eXp. The gentleman who introduced me to eXp has been there a year longer than me. He's been there two and a half years and he makes around $400,000 in passive income with rev share. I'm committed to that for my agents. I'm also committed to them building a business they're proud of. Aaron has been on the team almost eight years. This summer he's building a plan so that he can work all morning and then take all the afternoons off and go be in the garden. We'll see if that happens because I think we're built to work when we're in real estate. I'm sure he'll still pull some 12-hour days. Aaron got to spend all of February in Florida with his dad. I like that he gets to live that life. It's important for me and my team to live the lives we love.

LISA

How long ago did you join eXp? What company did you leave?

CHRISTINE

I joined in November 2019. I was with Keller Williams for 10 years before that. How long have you been with Sotheby's?

LISA

About eight years. I was with Prudential Douglas Elliman for 28 years and at another company for about 12 years.

CHRISTINE

How many of the million-dollar listing guys do you know from New York?

LISA

I bump into all of them. It's TV. It's all made up. When Frederick first joined Douglas Elliman, which is why he went over there to do this, the owner of Howard Lorber, his son Michael Lorber, worked for the company. They interviewed him. He had to take listings from other agents, pretend they were his and then pretend to do these negotiations. It was all pretend. A lot of established agents would never do reality TV.

CHRISTINE

You never know how they're going to twist it. You never know how they're going to edit it. They can make you look like a complete jerk if you're not careful. I would not want to do it. The editors could just out whatever they want and taint it and twist it any direction they want to go. Would you do it?

LISA

I don't like to be followed around and have every little thing I do recorded, especially in this environment. That would scare me. I would be afraid to say something I didn't mean and have it construed into something else. Then the more I try to defend myself, the worse I would look. That part of being on reality TV would scare me. As far as communicating value or knowledge or opinion, I could do that all day long, but I don't want to be part of some made up reality series.

CHRISTINE

Is there anything other advice you want to give to new team leaders or people who are going from the individual level to something bigger?

LISA

It's important to have good relationships with your fellow agents. When you're starting your career put money aside from each deal to invest in yourself and invest in your own properties. Put your money aside and invest in real estate, so you can achieve gaining passive income.

Lisa Maysonet leads the Lisa Maysonet Team at Sotheby's International Realty. As a real estate broker, owner, and investor for 40 years, her team members follow suit in experience, talent, and dedication. Their commitment to results comes with an exceptional approach to servicing buyers, sellers, and developers. To date, she has negotiated properties valued at over one billion dollars in the New York City metropolitan area. In addition to being an established top producer in the NYC market, her breadth of knowledge on real estate markets has expanded to include clientele from around the world.

TO CONTACT LISA

- lisa.maysonet@sothebyshomes.com
- 917.699.1050
- https://lisamaysonet.com/
- /lisamaysonetlivingnyc
- @groupmaysonet
- @groupmaysonet
- @lisamaysonet5724
- /in/lmaysonet/

SARAH RICHARDSON

AARON

Tell us about yourself and how you got started.

SARAH

I'm the founder and CEO of Tru Realty. We're an Arizona based independent brokerage. We've garnered our reputation from our education over the last decade. We are great at taking agents directly out of school and putting them through a training and a mentorship program that turns them into closers. The national average to get your first deal to escrow out of school is six to nine months.

43% of our mentees have their first deal in escrow within three months. We are exceeding the national average and getting our people up and running quickly. Our brokerage tends to be a bit younger, and our brokers are tech savvy and focused on education. Our median agent house is under 40 when the average of realtors is somewhere in the mid-fifties.

AARON

Tell me about the education program. What does it look like? Is it up on Kajabi? Do you do one on one mentorship? Is there a mentor that's accountable?

SARAH

Yes, to all the above. The agents are required if you've done five transactions or less to go through a three-week program. Sometimes we have agents who are struggling to get business do it, but it's made for the agents who are directly out of school. One hundred percent of the program occurs online in a Zoom like setting. This was something we did before COVID hit, so luckily, we were ready when it did. The program is held on Monday, Wednesday, and Friday from 10:00 AM to 1:00 PM. We record those sessions, so agents who are working part time can go back and watch them at the end of the day. The program goes over the fundamentals of growing a business, how to navigate through your MLS, how to negotiate and advocate in the purchase contract, what's in the purchase contract, and how to work with buyers versus working with sellers.

We go over what a fiduciary looks like, how to navigate and manage your database, how to work with vendors, what it looks like to juggle escrow, what communication looks like, how to comp a property, what your buyer presentation looks like, and what your listing presentation looks like. We go over the different ways of prospecting and then we end the three weeks with a business planning session where we map out the next 12 months for them. We look at how much time they have, how much money they want to make, and where their focuses are going to be. We don't want them to focus on all the ways we've taught them how to prospect. We want them to maybe pick two or three ways to prospect that resonate with them and focus on those. When they're finished with the three-week program, they enter a coaching, mentoring, and accountability program for 13 transactions.

Doing 13 transactions doesn't happen overnight. So, agents will remain in the coaching and mentoring program from six months to two years. They stay in the program until they can hit our highest split, which is at the 14th transaction. We're not sending them out in the world of real estate after that initial three-week program. We have different kinds of accountability forms. There are live coaching sessions, meetings, and other trainings we encourage. We can't force them to go through the 13-transaction mentorship and coaching program, but we encourage it. It helps them grow the backbone to get out into real estate and do what they need to do.

AARON

When you're in the mentor program, what's the split and how do they get out when they get out? How do you break that down?

SARAH

Their first three transactions are at a 65/35 split. For their next 10 transactions it's an 80/20 split. Then when they hit their 14th transaction it's a 90/10 split with a 15 cap. During those 13 transactions, live coaching sessions, tech training, conversion classes, overcoming objection classes, and business planning are all available to our agents.

CHRISTINE

You run a brokerage. Tell us about that. What's your favorite part?

SARAH

We have five teams. We have 120 million team, a 60 million,

a 40 million team. The brokerage has changed its form over the year. I was the designated broker for eight years. I loved the legal side and helping agents get their contracts accepted. Then we turned more to coaching and the tech side of things. Now it's all integrated. It's my passion to expand and help agents in Arizona and across the United States.

AARON

How many agents do you have in Arizona and where are you expanding to?

SARAH

We're expanding throughout the U.S. right now. We've got conversations going with several brokers of record throughout the U.S. Currently, we have a little over 130 agents and we've brough on several business development people in the last few months. Our goals are to scale quickly where we want and double in size. We're taking a bigger swing. Before. We always maintained between 100 and 125 agents the last five years. Now, we put people in the place to help us grow and expand a lot more.

CHRISTINE

Did you bring on recruiters?

SARAH

I don't like the term recruiter, and they don't either. We call them talent scouts. They are people who help us identify our core values and which agents fit into our growth mindset. We've always been a company of education and 80% of our agents have graduated into that 90/10 split. Because they've gone through the entire process, it's all about collaboration and giving back. So, we've hired talent scouts to help us bring on agents. We've built tech to drive traffic to attract people who are interested in our core values. It's important to find the right fit because everyone isn't a good fit. To find the right people, you must advertise, and market based on the people you're looking for.

AARON

You have part time agents and full-time agents. Is that normal for a broker? If they are a cultural fit, do they get to pick their own production level?

SARAH

We don't have any quotas for that. It can be difficult with new agents. We tested having a quota for a few years which was difficult because life happens. When you're working with a community of agents who are seasoned and have an established business, a quota is applicable, but when you're taking somebody that knows nothing about this and trying to mold them into a producer, you've got to be very gentle, loving, and caring. You must give back. It's a heroic thing we're doing because new agents are labor intensive.

CHRISTINE

Where do you draw the line if a person hasn't been producing for six months?

AARON

Where's the bottleneck for you? What is the hardest part of getting new agents to be productive.

SARAH

It's tough to know when to cut the cord. We've found they come out of the gate strong. They're excited but everybody knows about three people. Statistically, they get those first three deals done, they get to that 80/20 split, and they're excited. Then reality kicks in and we find that new agents are in a lull between six and 12 months. We're trying to get better at retention because it's hard to keep them motivated after six and 12 months and many of them want to quit all together or move to a different brokerage.

If they change brokerages, many of our agents come back. It's all about keeping them motivated and finding ways to switch their mindset and figure out what they are doing wrong. Maybe they need to reflect on their business plan or they're in a rut trying to revive their business. The biggest struggle we have with our agents happens at the six-to-12-month mark. Getting agents excited about selling real estate is an industry standard.

CHRISTINE

When they are outbid, lose a house, or lose a client, you must pick them back up off the ground.

AARON

The biggest hurdle we've come across is getting new agents to work eight to 10 hours a day finding business after they've reached out to all their low hanging fruit. The business of real estate is finding business. This isn't a hobby, it's a career. It's great they sold their mom's house but now they must go through 3000 people in a database, go door to door, or stand outside the supermarket. They need to be doing something with those eight hours to generate business.

SARAH

It sounds like you're really teaching them to grow their business. You're not hanging them a warm lead. You're training them on how to hunt.

CHRISTINE

Making those calls can feel impossible when they must speak to 40 people a day and it takes them two and a half hours to talk to 13 people and have been hung up on multiple times. People think they failed when they simply stopped.

Tell us about your special sauce?

SARAH

There is no special sauce. Some people think there must be a better and easier way to do this, and there's not. We have six ways to teach people how to prospect and they need to pick at least two of the six and rinse and repeat.

AARON

What do you mean when you say you have talent scouts in tech? I don't think there is any kind of tech that can replace people. Tell us about your tech.

SARAH

Our tech does not replace people. We use Chime for our CRM, and the agents use that as their CMS tool on their website. We beta tested Chime for them six years ago and I love that CRM. They have one of the biggest product roadmaps and probably the largest development team of any CRM in the real estate space. If you need something, they'll push out a new feature within five to seven days. That's unheard of in the tech world.

Chime is a great way to manage your database. It is robust on all fronts, text, email, and phone calls. It has all the integrations. We use a media company that integrates organically with Facebook, Instagram, LinkedIn, and Twitter. It's like the Hootsuite of residential real estate. This is the first Facebook and Instagram approved Hootsuite content calendar that allows your content to be seen. It doesn't mess up the algorithm, which is a big issue with some of those other content calendars. Our agents can create content for the whole year and then not think about it. Those are the kinds of tech tools we use.

We have a direct-to-consumer open house app. In Phoenix we are the hub of the IBUs down here. Opendoor offerpad and Zillow Instant Offer and they're all based here. There is a company that just launched in Phoenix called Zoodelio that is fabulous for teams and brokerages. Zoodelio is the first i-buying platform that empowers the agent, where other companies squeeze us out of the deal. Zoodelio is doing the same thing opendoor offerpad is doing but it's partnering with teams and brokerages to help them negotiate and earn a fee on top of that. It's a great way to get more signs in the ground. It's awesome that you train your agent how to hunt because many larger teams go the lead route.

CHRISTINE
We do have leads, but they're regular leads. They must go into the pond and go fish if they want them. We do a pipeline review once a week where we hold a public Zoom meeting and go over how many contacts they made, how many dials they did, how many texts they sent, and how many open houses they had. Then it's obvious what that agent needs to work on.

We can point out when they just gave up for the day. Once we have someone in our database, we put them on a drip campaign.

AARON

Is there anything you recommend for talent scouting?

SARAH

It's all about knowing our core values and our value prop on education. We want to be enmeshed at our local schools. Our biggest successor has been partnering with some of the larger schools. We don't want to become a school because that is another business itself. It's great to partner with them, however, and become the best candidate for after school in people's eyes. Partnering with schools has been huge for our business.

AARON

Do you have any books you would recommend your agents read? Are you reading anything right now?

SARAH

As a business owner, I've grown in the last decade. I've owned this company for 11 years and I've reinvented myself probably 10 times. *Traction* by Gino Wickman is one of the books that changed my life as a business owner. It can be applied to teams, team leads, and their business. Learning the EOS system is big. I'm in a group called entrepreneur organization. It's been helpful to be in a group with other business owners who are industry agnostic. *Traction* is good at helping you create processes. Organization growth is always part of a business plan and this book helps you put people, processes, money, and execution into play, so you can grow your business successfully. *Traction* is one of the best business books I've ever read.

Sarah Richardson is one of the preeminent leaders of residential real estate in the country. As CEO and founder of Tru Realty, she is responsible for both the daily operations and oversight of multiple growth strategies the brokerage carries out. In 2010, Sarah launched Tru Realty to better serve a marketplace that was seeing a shift from auction-centric fix/flips to an MLS flow. With an inspired vision to be a leader in residential real estate, Sarah built a strong and dedicated team who closed an astonishing 450+ deals in the brokerage's first 6 years of operation. What's more, nearly every deal was profitable, yielding double-digit returns.

Since Tru Realty's inception, Sarah has performed a variety of tasks, including but not limited to, recruiting, marketing, training, tech implementation, and more. In 2017, Sarah was the first realtor in the U.S. to execute an investor cash transaction on the Blockchain (using the Ethereum protocol) in partnership with Propy, one of the brokerage's key tech partners.

Born and raised in Waukesha, Wisconsin, Sarah moved to Arizona in 1996 where she attended Arizona State University (ASU) and studied Business Communications. In 2003, she shifted from her corporate path into real estate and became a member of the National Association of Realtors.

TO CONTACT SARAH

- ✉ sarah@buytru.com
- 🔗 https://trurealty.com/
- Ⓕ /trurealty
- ⓘ @tru_realty
- 🐦 @trurealty
- ▶ @Trurealty
- 𝗶𝗻 /company/tru-realty/

NICK GOOD

AARON

All right. Let's talk about Nick Good. He's the team leader of the Good Home Team. He's also the co-host of the only real estate podcast worth listening to, which I don't agree with, but nonetheless, he is the podcast host for the only real estate podcast worth listening to.

Nick's got a great story. Nick started in 2005, and it's a real rags to riches kind of deal. He really stumbled away around, almost took a regular job, you know how it goes.

Then something clicked for him and he really has been rocking the Dallas Fort Worth market since then, really since 2009, when it all clicked for him.

He's focused on hiring and developing leadership and systems. He is a systems guy, and he really gets in depth with his splits and how they run things and you can hear and everything he says, just how flat footed he is about the building of the systems. They've got a rocking team there now doing 200 transactions, $500 million a year.

We really welcome Nick to the show! Give us some background where you are, how big your team is, when you got started, just some background so people listening can get some context.

NICK

Yeah, absolutely. First off, thanks for having me, Aaron. So I'm here in Dallas, Texas. Born and raised in Dallas. I have my wife and three kids and a dog that's going through chemo treatment right now in McKinney, Texas. And my primary team is here in the Dallas Fort Worth, Texas area.

I also have a team in Austin and a team in Houston and been doing this, got in it unlicensed in 2005. Got my license in 2006 while still working as an assistant. And before it was called this, I was basically there showing an assistant to an independent broker. 2007, I graduated college, got married, bought a house and thought, hey, why not become a full time, 100% commissioned real estate agent all within pretty much the same month?

Go big or go home. The main thought process behind it was when I graduated college, the broker and said, hey, we love what you do. We want to offer you a salary position plus overrides. And I was like, I appreciate that, Jay. I love working here, but I see how much money you guys are making, and I would love to earn that type that type of money. Do you think I can make six figures just going 100% commission? He's like, absolutely you can.

So I was like, cool, I want to make six figures.

AARON

That's always a number that everyone picks when they get started.

NICK

Exactly. And that was my number in 2007. And I only sold three houses.

Back then, before our prices shot through the roof, I will tell you, like, I think our average sales price was $180,000, so I didn't make $100,000. And what I learned in this business was in 2007, when I was going through this, I'm 24 years old, and my friends were still in college or they just graduated and they were broke. And so the last thing that was on their mind was buying a house, right?

And the last thing that I could do, and this was my limiting belief, more than likely, because I didn't have the confidence, is I did not believe that my friend's parents were going to use their broke kid's friend. And so what I had inside of me, though, was I did not want to be seen as a failure to other people. I said, Man, I'm doing this real estate thing. I want to get into real estate investing. And so at the end of 2007, I knew I needed to change.

Then in December of 2007, I joined Keller Williams because I had a friend who took her real estate license at the same time, and she was having success.

And I was like, Aaron, man, knowing this friend, I love her to death, but if she's somehow having success, what's wrong with me?

Why am I not having the same success? It's got to be because it's the broker she's with. So she recruited me over to Keller Williams. I joined and started just to plug into what they were saying, just being around the people that were selling houses. And in 2008, I started getting some momentum. And for the first five months, first five or six months, was doing fairly well. Consistently starting to learn how to lead, generate online. I was using Craigslist, and I stumbled into selling some retirement active adult retirement homes.

I'm 25, and I can't even remember I stumbled into it. I wrote a blog on Active Rain, and it just kind of just kind of gained momentum from there. And in one month I can't remember what month it was, I'd really have to go back and look at this. I had eight pending contracts, and I was walking around like Superman. I was like, all right, I've got all this money about to come in. I'm ready to already I'm mentally spending it. Thank God I didn't run up my credit card because all eight of them fell out.

AARON

Nice, right?

NICK

And during that time, that's when the Enron thing happened and the financial collapse just came barreling down. And this is the first and only time, knock on wood, that I lost eight contracts in one month, and I was not able to revive any of them.

AARON

Oh, my gosh.

NICK

Right? Because people were losing their retirement stocks everything was just in the toilet. People were losing their jobs. And so I didn't know what to do, man. So I started to really get down on myself, just kind of mentally and started doing what normal people would do. I was like, all right, I'm going to go.

I'm thinking I'm probably not cut out for this 100% commission crap. Yeah, I started looking for jobs, so I start going and interviewing for jobs. And I land a job interview at an asset management company that was hired on to dispose of all the foreclosures that were starting to pile up. And so I go through the two or three interviews, and they said, Nick, we like what you have to offer.

We want to offer you a position. Awesome. I really need it. So they offered me, like, 60 or $65,000 a year salary. Again, I wasn't having anything coming in. And that was definitely at that time at 25, that's a nice little salary paycheck. And they're like, you need to work Monday through Friday, or really it's Monday through Saturday. And in order to hit the bonus level, you really need to work on Sunday.

And then when I calculated, I'm like, I need to actually squeeze an 8th day in there to really hit their bonus levels. And I said, okay, Aaron, I definitely appreciate it, buddy. Let me go home and talk to my wife before 100% coming into this. So can I call you back tomorrow? And I said, absolutely. On the way home, I'm driving home, and something just smacked me in the face. I had this, like, epiphany light bulb moment, and I was like, all right, if I were to commit the amount of time they want me to work here into my real estate business, can I make more than the 60 or $65,000 that they're offering me and control my outcome? I was like, absolutely.

And what really smacked me in the face is that I was expecting full time income on part time effort.

AARON

So good that you say it, Nick, because that's what we get all the time with our new agents. We got to get them to get if you want to work 40 hours a week, you need to work somewhere else. You need to work for someone, because this is a startup. You're a startup. You got to be like, you can work whatever 70 hours a week you want, but if you're not doing 70, it's not going to start. Your business is not going to start. So it's great. I'm really glad you said that.

NICK

Absolutely. And so after that Epiphany moment, I turned it down and I went to work. I started studying at the time YouTube was coming on, and I started studying some people that luckily were putting out their cold calling, their FSBO scripting, and just started to really understand that my sphere wasn't at a place to reap the rewards from yet. So I needed to go out there and prospect and lead generate for strangers, people that didn't know me yet and get them to eventually believe in me and trust in me. And so it was through trial and error started for selling my owners and then started dabbling or started mimicking and studying what the top agents were doing.

I was like, all right, if we're looking at the lowest hanging fruit, these are the people raising their hand. They're already willing to pay a commission. I don't have to fight commission amount. I just need to get them back on board to sell and say the reason why I didn't sell is probably the agent's fault or whatever it was back then. And so I just got on to calling and mimicking and not reinventing the well and duplicating.

And to make a long, long story short, from 2009 to today, I've made no less than six figures and now earn in the seven figure range. And it all started with turning down the job, understanding that I'm not going to make full time income on part time efforts, and that we're not here to reinvent the wheel. Right? It's already there. Let's just duplicate it, put a little bit of our spin on it, our characteristics, our charm, and our culture, and then we can grow something that's bigger than ourselves.

Today, we sell a little over 200 houses a year, consistently 60 to 65 million. And going up, we have somewhere around 15 agents on the team, 400 agents in my Downline organization here at eXp and Growing. And now the way the organization looks, I just hired team leader director of sales who runs our entire organization, and her role is to attract agents, recruit agents to the team and get them into production and growing their production.

AARON

That is dynamite. That's a great story, and I really do appreciate you going through the history of that, because I think for a lot of team leaders watching or listening, that's the kind of conversation that we get to have with our new agents is the thing about expecting full time pay off, part time results.

And what is full time and what is part time, especially in the beginning, what are you expecting?

Talk to me a little bit about the 15 people. Are they listing agents, showing agents, same.

NICK

Everyone does everything.

AARON

Tell me how they get paid, what's the deal?

NICK

Yeah, absolutely. Great questions. So I'm going to take you backwards in order to then take you forward. So when I started the team, obviously it was just me. It was just me and my brother. And as we grew and started getting success, is that we ran a traditional real estate team meeting. My agents that came aboard could only work one specific group, which was buyers. I was the listing agent. My agents that came aboard would only work the buyers.

If their buyers needed to sell, I would work that listing and they would not get paid on it. That works in the beginning, right? Because I didn't know what I didn't know, and I had to learn and evolve and grow. And so as I'm growing, you've got to find your lead levers or your lead mechanisms that are going to be consistent, and that's reproducible. You don't have a business or a system unless it's duplicatable by others.

So if you stepped out, Aaron, and it all falls apart, then you don't have a business, man, right. From 2009 till 2015, it wasn't a business, it was me. Everything revolving around me. I was the sun. If I went out, if my flame went out, the whole business goes under. And so as I'm running three to five listing appointments a day, because our lead generating mechanism, our bread and butter, has expired listings, what I noticed, what I came to a conclusion on, is that, one, I was starting to lose talented agents that wanted to list properties.

So I was like, well, no, you can't do that. That's my job, right? It was a very greedy and selfish model. And the light bulb moment on that is, as you grow into these roles, you'll start noticing there's always a light bulb moment that smacks in the face. Usually it's painful, and it's not always fun to experience at the time, is that I started losing talented agents that were going elsewhere and having success, and it was all because I was restricting them and not allowing them to grow and flourish under our team.

Then in 2015, I went from a standard model to our agents, what we call the hybrid model, where our agents could work both sellers and buyers. And we've evolved into that ever since. We've never changed it. It's been an amazing tool and amazing system.

It works like this: when our agents come aboard on the buy side, our commission splits are 40% to them if it's a team generated lead, 60% to the house.

If it comes from an open house, from their past client or their database, it's a 50 50 split.

AARON

Great.

NICK

We used to have increasing splits and everything else like that. What we've noticed in the past is that we need to keep our cost of sale between under 55%. Our job as a team owner and our responsibility, especially if we have employees, is maintain profitability. And also as a team owner, we're not here to make less money. We're here to also enjoy and reap the rewards of helping grow and develop our future leaders. But we're also here to do it profitably, not a nonprofit.

I see a lot of teams that come in and they start to overpay commissions. And the only way that that team is profitable is because they're not profitable because of the agents. They're profitable because the team lead is still in production, and they're doing all the production just to survive. And so I always warn people, it's like, just be careful on how your splits are. Don't sell on splits.

Don't sell on leads. Sell on the value and the growth and the leverage that you could help get them. Great. 40% to the agent on the buy side, 50 50 if it comes from their sphere, open house or past client.

On the listing side, we work it a lot different. On the listing side, it's 25% to the agent if it's a team generated lead, or 35% to the agent if it comes from an open house, past client, or from their database.

And the reason why these splits look different is because once our agents take the listing, they're 99% hands off. Our listing department does the rest of the work. Meaning from the day the listing agreement is signed here, they upload it in our system. Our listing coordinator calls and reaches out to the client, thanking them and resolidifying the great decision they made in hiring us and the good home team of getting their property sold.

Then we scheduled the photographer who's on staff. We have an on staff photographer and videographer. He takes the sign and lockbox out. We'll take the photos and videos of the house, and then we list the property. Now, once we put it on the MLS and start marketing the property, our agents can elect to do open houses or they can open it up to the rest of the team for the team to get the open house opportunities on it.

From there, once we get an offer, our negotiation, our licensed negotiation expert takes the offer, presents it to the client, and then goes over whether we need to counter it back or is it something that's acceptable, is it a great offer right now? So she will take it either through counters negotiations or acceptance stage. Then her job is also to get it through the repair negotiations because a lot of times, especially as we're coming back into a more normalized market and more inventory coming on, one of the number one reasons why terminations were to happen once a property went under contract was over disagreement and repairs.

Her job is to get it through that and then also to get it through closing. And then our agent shows up to closing and they have already prepped the client and we've already prepped our client on this, Aaron. They're going to ask for three things when they get to closing. They're going to say, Aaron, we get there. First off, I want to make sure you have a big smile on your face because, buddy, you're going to get a big old check deposit in your account and that's going to feel really good.

So when I get there, I want to make sure you're looking good, comb your hair, wear your Sunday best, if that's the case, because we're going to take a photo for evidence of success. We want to let everyone know that we didn't just say we're going to get the job done, we got the job done. So we're going to take a photo, possibly a video testimonial interview. Then we're going to ask for two things. We're going to ask for a review because we want to make sure we reach out to a lot of clients like yourself who may not have known about the good home team in the past.

We want to make sure that our current and past clients are showing our reputation. So if you can leave us a five star review, if it's anything less than five stars, please let me know so we can correct it and make it right. And then the last thing that we're going to ask for is we want to work with more clients like yourself. And when you make a move like this, you're going to become hyper aware. People around you are going to become hyper aware and may already probably consider making a move. So we want to work with your referrals. We want to work with people that's in your network that know like and trust and love you so that we can deliver the same results or better.

So our agents show back up at closing, do those three items, and that's the focus, right? And so the other thing as we get into a more normalized market is our operation and listings team also does the price adjustments talk because a lot of times, as you've seen, if you're newer or most agents in this market have been in the business, adjustments they're like, what is that?

AARON

The degree to which it's systematized is fantastic. It's flat. There's no questions when you open a satellite, this is how it's done. And that makes a big difference in the culture, because people agents are now not stepping into an experiment, they're stepping into a business. And I just know from our experience that that makes an enormous difference for an agent coming onto the team that they don't have too many options, too many things to think about, or too many changes.

People want to know that it is the way it is and it works the way it is. And then what do you do for training and development? How often do you meet? Give me the layout of what day looks like in terms of training development.

NICK

Yeah, that's our million dollar question right now. I'm glad you brought it up, because right now, today, we are going through and kind of updating that. So we meet every Tuesday over Zoom. Every Tuesday we do our team meeting, sales meeting, and we go over what's going on in the marketplace. We do a little bit of objection or role playing or how we can get clients excited about this evolving market that we're in. And so we do it once a week.

We use kind of two different channels. We use Facebook. Facebook groups. So we have a Facebook internal group that all of our agents in. And then we're starting to transition back over to Slack because we're starting to get more younger agents on our team. And what I'm noticing is that the young 20 year old agents, they're not on Facebook. So we're losing a way to get our messages out to them, to get them to plug into our team trainings and our team culture. So we're just trying to meet them where our agents are. So we're bringing Slack back in.

The way that it works right now for onboarding, it's not as clean as we would like it. So we're always looking at improving. And so right now, the way it works is we use loom. I have a 17 part video series that our agents go through in the beginning just to learn our systems and processes and our lead generation system website, which is Boomtown. And from there after that, then we jump either on a Zoom or in person to go over how we do our scripting, our sales processes and techniques in objection handling.

What we're looking at probably trying to go to is something more of a learning based platform. There's a company out there called Branded Agent University that we are really close to partnering with pulling the trigger on. And the way that it would work is every agent would get their login and then we would have our training or certification steps in there for them and we could see the progresses that they're making.

Every agent that joins the Good Home Team has the opportunity to become a Certified Home Buying and a Certified Home Selling Advisor through the National Association of Expert Advisors. Because of our partnership with Michael Reese and Jay Kinder everyone gets access to our Certified Home Selling and Certified Home Buying Advisor certifications. And so moving forward, that is going to be our continued onboarding training so that our agents can show they're the experts in the marketplace.

AARON

Fabulous. That's great. Again, you really just hear the confidence and the systemization of what you're building there. And it's obvious in your success that that's the way that's going. That's just dynamite. And again, I think before I started recording maybe or even whatever, the through line between the successful teams is always that sort of commitment to the development of the people and the systemization of the business. So just right on, I totally dig it.

NICK

I appreciate that.

AARON

Yeah. And Nick, first of all, is there anything else about your team that I didn't ask that you want to talk about?

NICK

I mean, really for us it's about putting the agents in the best position to win. So our belief when an agent joins us is from day one that an agent, whether they're brand new or veteran, has a seat at the table. They don't have to get phased in, they don't have to earn their way to certain lead sources so that they have the access from day one to the best systems, the best trainings, the best opportunities, the best legion, so that they can be put in the best position to win.

It's about them and their business and their families to be put in the best position to win so that they can choose the lifestyle of their choosing. When joining a team, a lot of times what ends up happening is we call it the parasitic team lead. And agents are actually competing for the scraps because the team leaders typically are cherry picking the best deals. And so what I always really warn future team owners and then even new agents that are looking to join teams is make sure to look at one, what is the success rate and the trajectory path for agents when they join a team.

Number two, are they competing against the team leader for business? Because if it is, what I've seen unfortunately is that team owners are going to get the best deals and they're just going to throw the scraps to their agents and that's not putting their agents in the best position to win. Again, our belief is our agents have to win. If our agents are winning the company is winning.

AARON

Yeah. That's great. Yeah. Neither Christine or I take any of the generated leads. I mean, we have our sphere leads, but we're not competing with them on those. But, yeah, I think that's a really universal principle for team leaders. I think probably at least half the team leaders I interview are out of production completely, so there is no competition. And the other half don't go through the same lead sources.

That's pretty much the way a successful team runs. And I think that's a really great universal principle to stand in is that you can't compete with your team and build your team at the same time.

NICK

Correct.

AARON

Great. Well, Nick, all right, so then just to wrap it up, what should I read? What's the next book that I should read?

NICK

I only read stuff that's a business builder. I like short books. For example, one is called the Legacy Selling System by Coach Michael J. Burt. And it's how to create more leads, build deeper networks, and close more deals. And then his follow up to it is million dollar follow up, a powerful seven touch system to get people off the fence.

He talks about that as real estate agents and sales professionals, we are leaving millions of dollars on the table by our follow up or lack thereof, and not providing value when we're with our follow ups, when we're making our follow up calls and we're lead generating, it's to be intentional. And it's intentional to bring them into a conclusion and a conclusion of them hiring you or not at that moment.

NICK

And it'd be like, Aaron, if I were following up with you, and I'd be like, hey, Aaron, I just got out of the shower, man, and I was just thinking about you. Have you decided to list your house? There's no value in that, first off. Or you've heard it like, hey, I was just in your neighborhood round the corner and just was thinking about you guys. Have you thought about making a move yet? There's no value in that. What are they going to say? Well, no, not right now. And so it's finding ways to create value when saying, hey, Aaron, it's Nick with the Good Home Team here, man. I was just wanting to touch base with you, see how you guys are doing, if you're ready to make that move yet. The market is starting to shift, but we want to make sure that we really capture your equity gains. And there's two things I was just thinking about you. One is selling this house. And also I wanted to invite you, you'd mentioned that you're interested in investing. We're running an investment webinar series on Wednesdays of how I've acquired over $100 million of asset holdings and have six figures coming in residual every year from that.

That's two things like where are you guys on wanting to sell that house? Are we ready to make a move on that yet? And then whatever the answer is. And then if I can get you on this investment training webinar that I hold on Wednesdays, I can only get 100 people on there and it fills up fast. If I could hold two spots on there, would you commit to showing up Wednesday at 10:00 a.m. Or whatever it is? Right.

And so we always go with an invite because we want that reason to follow up after and continue. And it's always inviting and providing value. Most agents don't provide value, and then we're not a valuable resource to our clients, then. Yeah.

AARON

It's great, Nick. Really great advice. And I appreciate the book referral. So give me something to check out next. Absolutely.

NICK

Thanks for having me on, buddy.

Nick Good founder of The Good Home Team - Co-Host on The Only Real Estate Podcast Worth Listening To, and is a top selling author. Nick entered the real estate industry in 2005, has sold over 3,000 properties, and has earned well over $6,000,000 in Commissions!

The Good Home Team has won the coveted Real Estate Team of The Year by Real Producers magazine and numerous other real estate awards. Nick can be seen on the national stage speaking at real estate events regularly. He is a trusted source for delivering inspirational and educational insights about team culture, leadership, and real estate marketing.

Nick's passion for helping others continues to drive him in his professional career, and he is committed to taking the real estate industry to the next level and inspiring others to achieve their financial dreams through an easy-to-follow blueprint that can guarantee an agent to make six figures! When Nick is not working, you can find him enjoying time with his family going skiing (or attempting to ski) or relaxing at their lake house.

Nick truly enjoys helping others become successful in life and business. So, if you are looking for a success story that shows what it takes to make it big in real estate then look no further because The Good Home Team has got you covered!

TO CONTACT NICK

🔗 https://www.nickgood.work/

TARA STONE

AARON

Today's show has got me super excited. Tara Stone is joining us. She is a New Jersey based realtor. She's a team leader. She is a successful business coach. She owns a vegan restaurant. She's worked all over the east coast. She is just brilliant with running a team, expanding a team, making a difference for people. She has a background in luxury and equestrian properties. Totally cool lady.

Why don't you introduce yourself to people, give us a little bit of your background, and then let's just jump in and talk about what you're doing that works on teams.

TARA

Awesome. Aaron, thank you so much for having me. I always try to put myself in a nutshell and it's never very successful. However, I've been selling real estate, 24 years transactionally across three different states and I started in commercial real estate.

AARON

Wait a minute. Wait. I don't know if some people are listening, but if they're watching this okay. How are you selling real estate for 24 years? Did you start when you were six?

TARA

Yes, exactly. I started when I was 21 and I'm 45 now. I grew up in construction with family and I really liked the commercial aspect of selling. My grandmother was a broker. I just remember from a very young age her saying, if you get your broker's license, that's something that no one can ever take away from you. So some family dynamics going on. We had, unfortunately, a lot of deaths in the family around when I was going to go away to college and I did not want to go away. Took some local community classes, got my cosmetology license. So I did hair right out of high school, which my high school was not happy about.

AARON

Wait, the high school cared what you did?

TARA

Oh, yeah. So big high school, they put on the bulletin board where everyone was going to college. And they called my mother and my grandmother into the guidance counselor's room and they said, you are letting her throw her life away. And they're saying this in front of me? Yeah. My head could not have hung any lower. But I wanted to be home. I wanted to be home with my family. And I've always loved helping people, and cosmetology was a way to do that. I liked making people feel good about themselves.

While it was a great experience, it was not long term for me. I had my grandmother in my ear, get your real estate license. Once I did, I never looked back. So started in commercial real estate along the 95 corridor in Connecticut, ended up selling luxury waterfront up in Cape Cod, Massachusetts.

AARON

Nice.

TARA

Got into bank owned work up there, then met my now husband whose brother was looking for a vacation property in Cape Cod. He bought it off of eBay, but they were using me as the local realtor to show them around. So the joke is, nobody screws me out of a commission. That's why I got his brother to marry me. We got married in the backyard of the house that he bought on eBay.

AARON

Right on!

TARA

Brought me to New Jersey, from Cape Cod to New Jersey as only love could do. And started in with bank owned properties, again here in New Jersey, but very different than the bank owned properties that were in Cape Cod, where I was really dealing with more of a second home market, a lot of vacant properties. And then I found myself in some of the more undesirable cities of New Jersey doing cash for keys, doing cleanouts.

And I think about six months pregnant. As somebody was chasing me down the road, banging on my car, I thought, maybe this isn't the smartest thing for me to be doing. Opened my own brokerage. We ended up moving. I had a very big, large niche, which I still have on equestrian properties and estates. Not everyone knows that New Jersey has more horses per capita than the state of Kentucky. I had a very happy bank account, very happy clientele. But I was ships in the night with my husband, and I had a two and a half year old who put both of his hands on each side of my face and turned my face and said, mommy, can you look at me?

And I was being the mom I swore I wasn't going to be. He had the TV and the iPad going. I am on my laptop waiting for my husband to get home so I can get back on the phone with clients. So I just stopped dead in my tracks, closed my brokerage, launched a Keller Williams office here in New Jersey, grew that from about 24 agents to 140 when I left three years later. Stepped out of transactional real estate altogether for about a year. I own a vegan restaurant that I opened during the time. It was a passion project for my son, and I was missing real estate terribly. I said, let me throw my hat back in the ring. I'll do a couple of transactions.

Now, three years later, I'm solely doing about 20 million, and I have a team of six that is growing and about 430 agents in what I would call our community across the United States and Canada with the coaching. So that's a nutshell.

AARON

That's awesome. That is quite the nutshell. I love it. I don't even really know where to start, but that's not true. Let's start somewhere. So tell me about you're with EXP and you have your own team, right?

TARA

Yes.

AARON

Let's just jump in with sort of the meat and potatoes of what I like to talk about on the podcast, which is what's working with your team, what do you do to train them? Do you focus on new agents? Do you recruit seasoned agents? Talk to me about the structure. Talk to me about your team.

TARA

Okay. And we talked a little bit pre call that we've been in a metamorphosis.

AARON

Oh, yeah. Tell me about the change. Tell me about what you were doing and what you are doing and what spurred on the change.

TARA

Yeah. I always say growth is messy and you want to break your systems. And I think EXP is a great example of kind of breaking its own systems. And that's a high level problem to have. As you're growing and learning and the market is shifting, we're always looking at what's the right thing for the team, not only specifically for the team members, but also for the functionality on longevity of the team. So commission splits training, what seats are on the bus, who are we looking to fill with those seats?

And with EXP, you have the standard commission, the

standard team, and then the self organized. So we do a little bit of both. We have a community that works well that anyone that comes into our revenue share line is welcome to come into our coaching, which we do every Monday. I have a Monday morning mindset. We have a group within workplace that people can engage in, and that's just agents doing their own business, living their life, collaborating with each other, coming in for the extra really coaching, because there's plenty of training and support when it comes to EXP.

AARON

Right. For people that are not in EXP, what's a self organized team?

TARA

OK That's really not even the self organized. That's just the community. Then we have the self organized team, and that's as we're rolling out more states. We're opening our basically what we've created here in New Jersey, we're starting to open it in other states. So that is there's going to be lead generation involved in that. You're going to get leads, you're going to have transaction coordination.

There's a whole other wall of value. And you can come in as a self organized team member where you're out doing your own business, but what you partner on with us, which is our leads and our process, then that's the team set up with that. And then of course, we have the Standard Team, which is really how we launched. And I do love the intimacy of that team, but I really view that team as a way for newer or less experienced agents to build their business, to learn how to turn that lead generation faucet up and down and take it to the next level. I think that the Standard Team doesn't allow the really talented go getters to see that big vision for the future. And it's one of the reasons I love EXP, because if you've ever trained an agent or brought an agent onto your team, the time, energy, effort, money, blood, sweat, and tears that you pour into them, if you're not in a model where they're going to outgrow you or they're going to want to start somewhere else.

That's why I like the Standard Team to really be, hey, I don't want you on the Standard Team for more than 24 months. You will always have a home on the Standard Team if that's just your thing. You don't want to lead generate, you rather pay a higher referral fee and you're just happy as a you know what pig. And you know what great. There's always a home for you. But really talented that people that are energized, that want to create a true career from this, 90% of them are not going to want to stay in the Standard Team structure. So I think it's very important that you create a very clear path and an expectation for what does it look like when you come on, where can you grow to and how can we do it all within our bubble of coaching, support, training, and growth?

AARON

Good. So talk to me about the Standard Team splits and the self organized splits.

TARA

Our Standard Team split was mostly falling at the minimum requirement for EXP, which is 25% to the team, and then they're on a half cap with an 80 20 split back to EXP. We were having the agents work their own leads. We use Ylopo and follow up boss. We also use KVCore. But we've had good success with Google AdWords and then we've taken a lot of our budget out of Facebook. We still do a little bit, but we're more focused on Google AdWords and retargeting the agents.

I think 5% of the population likes making cold calls. They would do it. It was becoming more of a big brother, almost like me pressing down, like, why aren't you following up? Did you make your call? That's not the position as a leader that I want to be in. Right. I'm not here to hold you accountable to your goals. I'm here to help you be accountable to your goals. So this is one of our big structures that we've changed that it's gone from a 25% cost to a 35% cost, but we're engaging an Isa, an inside sales associate, to work those cold, cool, and warm leads that are coming in and actually place appointments on our team member's calendars.

AARON

If an ISA books the appointment, the agent gets 65% correct. Got it.

TARA

Correct.

AARON

Listing or a buyer.

TARA

Yes. For the most part, there are some caveats to it for the luxury and the equestrian, because as a team, we pay for all transaction coordination. We pay for all of marketing, photography, video signs, lockboxes, you name it, because we have a team standard that we must meet. So if you have a new agent that doesn't have $1,000 extra laying around to do the marketing, we want to take that burden off of the agent, keep our standards in the team.

AARON

That's critical. Yeah.

TARA

So that's really where we've made a big change. We made a 10% change. And I was a little nervous about it at first because as an agent, you're going, oh, my gosh, I'm going to get 10% less. But everybody has been like, I don't have to make those calls all the time. Now I get just to get them booked into my calendar. And they're thrilled to have that. And they have the option if they want to show and prove that they can follow up with leads that are expensive.

And that goes to showing your work as a team leader. I think you need to share with your team the costs that are involved so that they understand the value of every lead that comes through. They've been happy with it so far. They are happy to not have to make those calls. Great.

AARON

How many people you got on that in the standard team?

TARA

We had seven, and we are at six right now because we had to make a departure with a relationship because it just wasn't meeting the team standards.

AARON

Good. Do you have team standards in terms of production, or is it culture or is it both or tell me about both.

TARA

Yes. And again, going to this point in time we're at right now, we are really digging a lot deeper into what the team handbook looks like. And my partner is very straightforward. He's like it's a handbook. That's what we call it, a handbook. I'm like, no, I want to be like the thrive guide. I want it to be something more fun so it's the handbook, but it's the team guide to thrive. It talks about expectations, talks about the standards, has initials on every page, has a signature. Because as a leader, again, you don't want to be policing your team.

AARON

Well, it's also their independent contractors. There's a limit to what you can right. But you can say, listen, these are the standards of the team. Do they have production quotas? What's the minimum for something else?

TARA

Literally hung up on that call this morning. I think it's very generous. It's one closing a month, and you're expected to have your first contract written if not closed within 90 days of starting with us.

AARON

That's great.

TARA

And that's accountability both ways. That's meaning that we're doing our job as the team to get you into that production and that you're showing up at a high level as well. So definitely two way street there.

AARON

Great. So just to be clear, Tara, I do this every time on the podcast, but those standards and that split generous. Little bit better than our team splits, really, and standard wise. So you're right in the we're joking pre call, like, am I doing this right? You are. That is and what's the self organized split? And how does that if someone's in Minnesota and they join your organization but they want to be in your mindset, group and do they pay a split?

TARA

No, they don't have to pay anything if they just want to come to the coaching. Now, if they want us to set appointments for them, it's 10% more expensive to them than if they were on the standard team. So the 35% goes to 45%.

AARON

They're not contributing regularly to the culture.

TARA

Exactly. But it's a win for a lot of the agents because they're either just starting out or they need to ramp up. And of course, especially with listings, the more buyers that bring. So it's worth it to them. And then looking around at the industry and what we're paying to Redfin and all of those, you're looking at

40% to 50%. And that's without any marketing. You're not getting transaction coordination, not getting any of those value adds. So I feel really confident in that.

AARON

And culturally, don't short sell the value that being with you makes.

TARA

Absolutely.

AARON

You attracted them for a reason. They're in your organization for a reason. They resonate. There's something there that speaks to them, and that's worth something.

TARA

Well, there's a value to that. Right. So I'm also a certified success coach, but I also work with success as one of their team coaches. So if you were going to hire me at a very basic level, it's $1,000 a month to coach with me. It's important that there's value there because otherwise people don't show up. But that is a great thing. You can pay $1,000 a month to coach with me one on one or you can have access to me once a week, and then I always make time for people that are within our organization if they need a little something more, but they're maybe not ready for one on one coaching.

AARON

And so talk to me a little bit about that. That's dynamite. I'm a coach and my partner is a coach, and we created a program to train our agents that we've opened to outside teams. And so talk to me about some of the principles or where you stand to coach your people, what makes your coaching valuable for people.

TARA

So it's really a very holistic approach. I've been there and done that, trying to compartmentalize work and family life and self care, and I've never had success with it at a high level. Something always ends up suffering. So when I go back to what I said earlier, we don't need more training. There is so much amazing training out there, and can I train someone? Yes. Can I get them into some of our courses? Yes.

But talking from my coaching hat, we're talking about mindset. We're talking about why are you really waking up every morning, unemployed, as a realtor, without health benefits, without all of any of the guarantees, really digging deep into why they got into the business, getting some blinders on. I find a lot of people just they're going through the motions. They're paying all the money for the lead gen.

They're engaging this system and that system, but they have very little clarity around what their standards are, around what their vision is for the future, for themselves, as a business owner, as a human being, as a mother, wife, husband, brother, whatever it might be, and looking at how can because I don't believe in a perfect balance. I believe we're always counterbalancing. How can we look at take stock of where we're at right now, where we want to make improvements, and maybe we want to make improvements in ten places. That's great.

We're going to be able to do that together in a coaching relationship, but we're not going to be able to do all ten at once.

AARON

Right?

TARA

So let's pick one or two. Let's get hyper focused on what the actions need to look like, what are your commitments around that, and then how can I help you be accountable to that? I don't, like, hold you accountable. How can I help you be accountable to those things? Because once you start really learning how to say no to the things that aren't moving your business forward, that aren't being run through that filter of your future vision, you get time back, you get clarity, you get the confidence to know that no is a complete sentence.

And you get to pour into the things that you're passionate about and that are moving you forward and are helping you show up as that person that you want to show up as to your team, to your family, to yourself.

AARON

That's awesome. It's so well said that no is a complete sentence. I love that part of our time. We have a conversation with people halfway through our training because it looks like to them they're getting stopped by time. And it's bullshit that they're getting stopped by time. You don't get stopped by time. There's no managing your time. There's managing your word. And it is very much a function of people inability or unwillingness. Not really inability. It really is an unwillingness to say no.

What I do from nine to twelve is I do lead gen. I don't answer the phone from nine to twelve. That's a no. This is what I'm doing now. Even just to say that this is what I'm doing now.

TARA

What you're committed to.

AARON

Yeah. And what's the action now that is going to move me a degree closer to fulfilling my ten year vision or whatever, who I am, my mission in life? And then it gives you a really easy way to say no to this and yes to this. Because it either fits or it doesn't. That's great.

TARA

And you're always saying no. Everything you say yes to, you're saying no to something else.

AARON

Yes.

TARA

So you're not avoiding saying no. You're just maybe saying no to the thing that's a little more forgiving, which tends to be our friends, family, and our own personal commitments.

AARON

Right.

TARA

Which in the long run are some of the most devastating things to say.

AARON

Or you're saying no to the thing that's confronting, like lead gen or, something like that, and that's the thing that's going to build your business.

What else is working for you?

TARA

We've tried virtual assistants. We've had some success with it, but it wasn't at the level that we were looking for. So we've identified people within our organization that excel at making calls, that will consistently make calls.

AARON

And you pay them for appointment setting?

TARA

Well, right now they're licensed, so they actually will get a percentage of every deal closed. And we're still looking at that structure. Is there going to be some bonus for appointment setting? Are there expectations for appointment setting? Yes, 100%. And to be totally honest, we're looking at those numbers right now.

AARON

Yeah, that's a tough one. We brought people in and exactly that. We stopped doing it because they wound up setting mostly FSBO appointments. And I just don't think you need someone to set you a FSBO appointment. I don't need to pay 15% of my commission to someone because they set me FSBO.

AARON

We haven't cracked the code on that. And I know there's a big market to sell VA services. Like, they can do that. I've had zero success in having a VA from another country call an expired and set a meaningful appointment on any kind of scalable basis. So maybe there's someone watching who've done that. You should contact me and we want to talk about it. Although my guess is if you found someone to do it, you don't want to share who that is.

TARA

I know a lot of leaders who are successfully using VAs. I'm a big believer in like if you're going to commit to something, a minimum of three months and really six months to really decide if it's something that works for you. And we went through a couple of different VAs and they were lovely people, but it just was not the right fit for us.

AARON

Yeah, and right fit. But I mean, look, if they were scheduling bookable appointments that converted, they would be the right fit for you. So let's not pretend they weren't the right fit because somehow culturally, no, they just weren't booking the appointment. So that deal with booking those appointments, those cold calls would be great to get that outsourced. I just have been completely ineffective at finding the right people to do it.

On one hand, it could be I haven't been willing to commit the six months I've done it for six months, but I don't know that I'm managing it the way it could be managed. Anyway, we're not doing it. If you crack the code on it, let me know. But we have had success in empowering our team to call the pond, to call those people, those leads that we do filter through Ylopo and Realtor.com.

TARA

I want to say your money is sitting you're here in front of me almost in tears because you don't have enough transactions closing yet. There's 60 leads sitting untouched right at your fingertips, but you don't want to pick up the phone and make the call. You'll send them a text, you'll send them an email, but you need to pick up the phone and call them. Your money is sitting right there.

TARA

Sometimes it's just those very candid conversations and I had to make calls in front of my mentor and he would have me put people on hold and I would be so shocked if they didn't hang up and be like, say this and do this. And we get so fearful, right? We're full of fear. We don't want someone to judge us. We don't want to fail all of this. Meanwhile, we're failing out of real estate at crazy levels as an industry because we refuse to pick up the phone and just start to create more relationships.

AARON

It's 100% it's a contact export. And look, you don't want to do cold calling, fine, don't. Then get yourself in five open houses a week, but you still have to pick up the phone and call the people you met at the open house. It doesn't matter how, at the end of the day, you don't want to do open houses, you don't want to cold call, fine. Stand out in front of a supermarket and hand out flyers for your first time home buyer class. But you still have to call those people.

There is no escaping. You need to talk to people.

TARA

Now, as we go into a shifting market. It's going to be more important than it has been in the last 24 months.

AARON

Totally. With you. 100%. And easier to talk to them about it, too. That's fabulous. It's great. All right. Well, Tara, I think we covered everything that I was excited to cover. Is there something I should have asked you that I didn't ask you?

TARA

No. I mean, there's so many great questions. There's so many great questions. I think the one thing I would just make sure that no one succeeds alone. Just no one succeeds alone. And whether you're a team leader or someone that's looking to get onto a team to maybe launch your business or reinvent your business, make sure you're coming with a mindset of abundance and with a mindset that you are going to be working together.

Getting back into these relational, face to face, person to person, real life humanity, that's, like, such a golden moment for me. And I really feel like that's where we are and embracing as many people as we can into that that are swimming towards the boat. You can't help the ones that are swimming away from the boat. But if they're swimming towards the boat and you've got a system and I know that there's opportunities for people that come on board with us, just like there's opportunities for us to bring these talented people on board. We're going to grow together.

I think it's an amazing time. I hear a lot of negative conversation out there. I've had some of my best years in down markets or changing markets or shifting markets, and the more that you humanize this process, the more fun real estate is, the more fulfillment that's going to come through, and we have to do it together.

AARON

Perfect. Tara. Thanks. All right, the last question I always ask is, what are you reading or listening to?

TARA

What should I read right now? I am reading no matter what. And those are the ten commitments of accountability from Sam Silverstein.

AARON

Oh, great. I love that name.

TARA

Sam is awesome. I am also going through a new certification, which is Certified Accountability Advisor, because I really believe that everything does exist just outside your comfort zone, but 100% within your accountability zone. There's no point to get uncomfortable if you're not going to have some accountability around it and actually make it happen. So I love that.

And Ryan Serhant. Big Money Energy. We call it BME. My team at least, I don't know, 100 times a week we talk about, hey, good morning. How's your BME today? Just bringing it, bringing that. Big Money Energy.

AARON

I love that. I love that acronym.

TARA

Thank you for having me. Great to meet you. Have a kick ass rest of the day.

AARON

Thanks.

Tara Stone is a modern day entrepreneur, with an impressive resume of successes. She works as a corporate coach for Nirvana Healthcare and as a SUCCESS coach. Her passion for business also spans to the vegan restaurant sector and luxury real estate, where she has not only been a successful broker but also a pioneer in bringing healthy plant based eating to her community. When she's not busy running her businesses, Tara is a devoted mom to her incredible son and an avid NJ Devils hockey fan. A sports car and Jeep enthusiast, Tara loves the open road and finding adventure in life! Above all, she is passionate about taking a holistic approach to living - from health to wellness to spirituality - finding counterbalance in every aspect of life.

TO CONTACT TARA

- Tara@TheDrivenAgent.com
- http://www.thetarastone.com/
- 908.923.3332 - Director
  908.348.8604 - Assistant
  908.209.9277 - Personal

JAMI AMIDON

CHRISTINE

Tell us, how many people on your team are you talking agents here?

JAMI

Well, I have one agent, so I pretty much worked as a single agent until the end of last year, and in August, I hired my first. I always had a TC, like, from the very first deal, because I hate paperwork. Honestly, I didn't even know how to get paid until about three weeks ago.

AARON

Christine's recreated in that.

JAMI

Yeah, not my thing. So anyway, I'm like, I need to leverage myself here, and hired a brand new agent just out of school. But she has a background, she grew up in the business, and her mom was a broker in Miami, and she has been amazing. And then I had the person who started with me when I very first got started, so I kind of did it a little backwards in entrepreneurship.

I think that systems give you strength. Like, structure gives you freedom.

I was coming into this, not knowing anything about this side of the transaction, I'm like, okay, I don't know what all this means. I was new to North Carolina, so all the laws are different, and I started putting my systems together.

I'm glad I did it that way. It was slower start to the business, but now it's like we are on the threshold of some explosive growth. We have found the right people on our team.

CHRISTINE

Right? Talent is huge, and I've probably been through eight TCS already. We found the most particular person on the planet because if I don't know how to get paid, you better know how I get paid.

AARON

So, Jamie, tell us about the project and tell us about Quantum Coaching and what you do to empower the people on your team.

JAMI

Okay, well, I started Decide to Fly in 2012. I was in the mortgage industry in Tucson and I hated mortgages. They were stressful. I found like everyone was lying everywhere, you know what I mean? These no Doc 500 FICO loans were in existence everywhere. It was just like, this is a big nightmare. And so it was like, the more you know, the more you don't want to know. You just put your head down and like, I'm just going to go to work.

I just had to get out and wound up with cancer in my eye, actually. And I felt like it was God's way of saying, you know, you need to take another look at your life.

That's when I decided I was going to really do something to empower women. I put a date on the calendar, and it was like Father's Day and this event happened. We had 202 women at the Ritz Carlton.

AARON

I can't believe you filled that yourself with 200 people.

JAMI

It was like I got on the phone, blah, blah, blah. I'm calling all my leader friends. I'm like "you, bring the tables" and "you come and do this."

And I'm sitting there maybe two weeks, three weeks before the event, and I'm like, "what am I doing? I need to sell something at this event or it's going to be a giant, expensive debutante ball."

Like, here I am, but I don't know what I'm doing. So I found somebody who was an online marketer, and how do you get the word out and all of that.

She was amazing. And I realized it's like, you know what? There's something really deeper to this for me. So I put together a program, and it came from a grief loss recovery course I had done. I had a certification in that. And then I went to Landmark.

CHRISTINE

So when you were talking about all the mortgages where you put a mirror under their nose, if it fogs up, give them a loan. Was that before the 2008 crash or after?

JAMI

It was before.

CHRISTINE

Wow.

JAMI

That's why I got out of the business I just said, I have to figure out something. So actually, I think I got into a multilevel skincare company, and it became a top 1% producer in that company. And that just wasn't what my future was going to be. I just knew it. And I don't know, I just wanted to help women. And so I created a course, and it was just like a culmination of lots of different things that I had grown through over the years.

And we launched it. Honestly, it was a financial failure. I'm just going to say what it is. It was a financial failure. I did not know what I was doing. What I was doing was spending a lot of money. I had this vision for the technology that would support it that wasn't in existence at that time, and it was running side by side with people, tech companies who were creating it.

By the time I was ready to launch, I had spent probably like 400 grand or something insanely stupid on all of these, because you're in it, you're deep and you're like, okay, what do I do?

Put another 50 grand in because I'm halfway in, I'm not going to keep going.

I learned a big lesson. Do stay in your lane. Do what you know or what you're passionate about. Don't do what you're not passionate about. I was not passionate about technology. You know what I'm saying? So anyway, I ended up connecting with C suite women executives across the country, and I've been coaching women like that ever since. And right now, it's by referral. The Quantum Shift coach is actually through a friend of mine who her business is to support Naturopathic Doctors. And so she called me up a couple of years ago and said, hey, will you coach some of my clients?

And I agreed to do that. So that's actually what that is. So I've got Naturopathic Doctors that I'm helping build their businesses across the nation. And really, it boils down to the same conversation.

AARON

Totally.

JAMI

It's the I'm not good enough conversation, right? Like, we got to complete the past.

CHRISTINE

So you can do transformational coaching. It doesn't matter which industry.

JAMI

Not at all.

I remember a conversation you had one time, it was about the invisible. Like, you're dealing with the invisible as if it's real, right? It's really not real. It's made up, it's not real. And I'm like, oh, my gosh, that was life changing for me. It was amazing. It was amazing. I have this little thing on my board here. It says, numbers are no judgment of who I am, just a gauge of how I'm performing.

AARON

Isn't that great?

JAMI

Brilliant.

CHRISTINE

Yeah, brilliant.

AARON

For people, that's life changing to get that. And that's the only thing we should be talking to people about. "That's your performance", and then "what are the actions you're going to take?"

And then who is going to be the person that's going to take those actions? Who would you need to be to take those actions effectively so much?

JAMI

Because it's like we walk around with, I'm wrong, or I should have, I could have, I would have. What if it does? What if it doesn't? All of those things, it's like that's just mind numbing. It's like, gosh, when you step across that threshold, you break through that. It is like life explodes. Right. You really start to get a feeling for what it's like to live life, and we're not even there yet.

CHRISTINE

Live life being cause in the matter of life. Not being a victim of whatever. And it's like you said, it doesn't matter what the industry is. We're using real estate, but it could be anything.

AARON

Jami, tell me about your expansion plans and how you compensate your people.

Just because I know one of the things that's sort of a taboo. We don't talk about compensation, but it makes such a difference for other team leaders to hear. Okay. That's what they're paying. Because every time we do this, we're like either, oh, my God, we're right on track. This is like or we learned something new. Right. Or we're like, wow, maybe we're paying them too much. I mean, it's just useful to compare notes. So you just brought on a new agent.

You have an Isa. What do you pay them? How do you pay them? Where did you find them? Everything we can know about how you got your team set up.

JAMI

Okay, so I started with the transaction coordinator, and that was an outsource. So that is anywhere between $350 and $400 a transaction. And that worked for me because it was my pace, one at a time, blah, blah, blah.

But I really wanted to bring that on in house and then have them help me with some admin stuff and listing all that kind of junk. I need to have somebody side by side with me. So I have Aubrey now who has taken on that role. She just started about a month ago, and she is doing great. So she takes everything from beginning all the way to compliance and is learning.

I created, like I said, my systems, they're all on Asana, and we use Asana as our boards. They're just dialed in very detailed. We use our own command, and then I have follow up boss as our CRM. I really only use Keller William command for compliance. It's too big of a monster to try to tackle anyway. So the transaction coordinator was the first person I hired. Like I said, I just needed somebody who was maybe a little bit smarter than me in the contracts on that side. So that worked pretty well.

AARON

Somebody to keep us out of jail.

JAMI

Yeah, exactly. So Sarah is now my Isa, and she lives in Austin. She's remote. She's also ops. Her gift is Ops.

I have this thing that I do. It's like a love hate list. So tell me everything that you love and everything you hate to do, because we really want to do what we love when we're working, right? I mean, we spend most of our day doing that.

Let's put you in the lane that you love, and if there's somebody else on the team who loves what you hate, then you can just cross. I don't care what your role is, just let them do it. As long as we get to the result at the end, that's super great for me.

Sarah is just a natural. She ran 17 restaurants in Austin.

CHRISTINE

I love that.

JAMI

Yeah, she just is just amazing. And she actually was the very first person I hired that helped me get these systems together.

And she was in between jobs, and I said, Sarah, please come move in with me because I was working out of my home. So she literally did.

And she worked with me for, like, eight months to get all my I mean, we took all of the best of the best from the mega teams in our company, and then we just picked through everything and we made it ours.

R and D rip off and duplicate. Just made them great. And she was so proud of us. Two years later after because that was a temporary thing, two years later, she's like, you're still using some of this stuff, and it doesn't even look the same. It just looks elevated.

We took all of that and grew with it, she came back on.

Now she is just getting trained for Isa.

Like I said, all of these people are kind of new. Again, Sarah was a top producer. She actually was in the car business. I said, "If you can be the number one car salesperson after four months, you can do Isa."

I told her, "You're coming here and I'll grow fast enough to cover your salary."

We'll transition into per qualified lead, per closing. But I need to give her some ramp up time, and I am paying her a set salary weekly for the Op stuff. She's very good at delegating her time.

CHRISTINE

Well, you said you wanted to duplicate yourself, so you got an agent to take some of the real estate.

JAMI

Yeah. So she was the first hire.

I have a VA. I hired an out of country VA. And I love him to pieces, but my personality is somebody that I just need to point you in the direction. Here's all your resources. Figure it out. I am not the person who's going to train you well.

I'm just not that temperament. I need somebody who is like Sarah, who can just take it and organize it, tell me what to do, because I just want to be on the phone making phone calls and doing that kind of thing.

CHRISTINE

Aaron's got this funny look on his face.

AARON

What's? Don't interpret my face. I'm loving this. I'm sitting here thinking this is the conversation.

The person we found is Maddie. She is our director of operations, and she's brilliant. And Maddie and I were talking yesterday about the problem we have with offshore VAS, that you literally have to sit with them and train them, and it's just insanity to do it. I must do it myself.

And then we need someone in video that speaks English, but doesn't just speak English, like can watch a video and get the point of what is in the video and how to edit it so that it's compelling.

CHRISTINE

That kind of storytelling.

AARON

We don't have to send it back four times like we just did.

JAMI

That's a bit frustrating, I have to admit.

AARON

Brilliant at some things. They are brilliant entry and fixing my website, right?

JAMI

Yes. And so we've kind of put them on. I have a contract with that company until June, and we'll just have to evaluate May.

CHRISTINE

What's the company? What are you using for the outsource?

JAMI

MyOutdesk. I really love the human guy as a human being like I really do, and it's going to be heartbreaking if we don't keep him. So we're trying to find something for him to do. But I just heard you're not being heartless when you're making those tough business decisions. You're just making them with less heart. Do you know what I mean? It's like you can't even know that.

CHRISTINE

That's true. You have to be smart about it. Our previous director of operations I had for seven years. She was brilliant. Aaron tells me the same thing, "Christine, anything is possible, but not when you're hiring. If they can't do the job, you got to let them go." Because I'll hold on to people because I like them, even though I.

JAMI

That'll kill your business. Your bottom line. Elizabeth was hired as a new agent, and I envisioned having kind of a customer service manager or client care coordinator kind of thing, where we did our buyers consultations together. You get two agents for one. Elizabeth and I go out there, maybe the first two showings and Elizabeth takes it on.

I taught her side by side how to have the conversations and do that for a good August through this month.

She was on salary, so we paid her a salary, and then I paid her 5% of whatever she touched, and it was a small salary.

She was out there running to and from the attorney's office because we're an attorney state, picking things up, making sure that all of our marketing looked great. Amazing at it. Just gifted.

And when I started to just really look at my bottom line again, it's like, okay, now I've got all this staff. I need agents, we need to produce.

Elizabeth is going to start producing on her own in March. Yeah, she's great. And we will be hiring two more agents. We're a pretty small team. I mean, my goal this year is 75 deals, so it's pretty low, but I think it's going to be a great year.

CHRISTINE

Awesome for you. Extraordinary.

JAMI

We're going with the right people.

CHRISTINE

You're growing organically by what you need now versus just trying to put a square peg in a round hole.

JAMI

Yeah. We started doing team meetings on Thursdays, and I'm loving them. I literally wake up and love Thursday because it's our team meeting and we're working through the five dysfunctions of a team. Have you read that book?

AARON

No.

JAMI

Oh, my gosh. It's a great book. Yeah. You got to read that book.

I read it years ago, too, and then I just pulled it back up and I'm like, you know what? We're going to do it. It's really about building trust and authenticity and awareness. Yeah, it's great.

Communication and just really getting that people have each other's backs, that we're not working against each other.

But the very first sentence in the book, it's not about strategy, it's not about money, it's not about any of that. It's about what makes successful team is the team itself – it's all about culture.

CHRISTINE

We always felt like if you get the right people, you'll find a seat for them on the bus which is from Tom Collins, Good to Great.

JAMI

It's so important. Exactly. Which is why, like I said, I'm a little over leveraged right now for myself, but I know it's not going to be that way. Probably by May we'll be awesome. Flip the thing over.

CHRISTINE

Great. Well, Jamie. What other books? Because that's usually how we wrap it up. Yeah, I love Five Dysfunctions of a Team.

Any other books you recommend? Any other books you're reading now?

JAMI

Yeah, I'm reading this book called Quantum Success the Astounding Science of Wealth and Happiness by Sandra Anne Taylor. And this I've had my coaching clients read this book, too. It makes you think, and we all know that thinking is a good thing.

I love that what we've created is coming from my calling.

It's just such a different way to do real estate when you are coming from your calling. And my calling is people are connected to love.

When I look at our commitments for the team and what we're all about, and we all pulled together words that described what a luxury experience at every price point is, we described what connecting hearts and homes means to us, each one of us, and it's present. It's present. And it makes me love my job. And this is a brutal market, so you better love your job. Right?

CHRISTINE

A lot of work.

JAMI

It's insane out there.

CHRISTINE

Jamie, thank you so much for your time.

JAMI

Awesome. I love it. All right, you guys.

The idea of home - how to find it, create it, and enjoy it - has been **Jami Amidon's** passion all her life.

How to create home originally began when Jami opened an award-winning home accessory store in Tucson, Arizona with $1000! Long story here⋯! For many years, she curated the best local and national decor, paintings, and gallery items. She brought people things that would bring them joy in their homes as they created a space that was uniquely theirs. The store garnered several local and national articles and accolades.

How to find home started with Jami's entry into this industry as a Lender in 2001 and now she's in the Top 10 Realtors in the largest Keller Williams office in Raleigh, NC. Connecting Hearts and Homes by collaborating and creating possibilities for her clients in real estate has developed into a true passion for the industry.

How to enjoy home is the personal journey that became a women's mentoring community called Decide To Fly. Focusing on foundational growth is key in creating a life you love.

Jami Amidon is paying her good life lessons and experience forward into her following generations. She and her family love living in the Raleigh area, enjoy everything local, and continue to share the discovery of finding homes that feel "just right" for her clients and all the life they're wanting to live.

TO CONTACT JAMI

- ✉ Jami@ForSaleInTheTriangle.com
- 🔗 https://www.jamiamidon.com/
- 📞 919.897.9494
- ⓕ /forsaleinthetriangle
- ⓘⓝ /in/jamiamidon/
- 🔗 https://linktr.ee/jamidon

BRETT ROSENTHAL

AARON

Okay, well, Brett, thank you for being on the show. We're looking forward to hearing all about the team you're leading at Compass and how you got started and that whole deal. So thanks for making the time to be on the show.

BRETT

Thanks for having me.

AARON

You're welcome. All right, well, let's just jump in. So we were talking pre show a little bit about your background. Never wanted to be a Realtor, but then someone put a gunny sack over your head and you woke up in the middle of the testing. And what happened?

BRETT

How did you know?

I could go way back, but basically I grew up in a family with parents that were Realtors and it used to occupy my family dinners and I never wanted to be a Realtor. Then in high school, I was lucky enough to be given the part time job of working at my parents' real estate office back before we had computers, answering calls.

And what happened was the Realtors that were calling, I didn't ever want to deal with again. They were mean, they were rude, and I was just a young high school kid answering the call, trying to set appointments. Didn't want to go into real estate. I ended up being a lawyer. I worked at the public defender's office in Philadelphia. I loved it, found out it didn't pay a lot of money, then moved to New York City and did real estate law.

More like the bankruptcy and the foreclosure. I didn't like that. And somehow I got involved in sales, like telecom sales back when it was, like, booming and I was horrible at it and got hooked up with a team where everybody was horrible, everybody was new, no one knew what they were doing, and somehow we all got it to click at once. And that's when I learned, like, if you're on a team where everyone's trying new and even if they're screwing up, you can make something good out of it.

AARON

Good, because that's the other thing you were talking about is how you like training people. So how did that influence your training?

And talk to me about how you were saying preshow that you love new agents. Which is I think it's more common than you think it is. Every team would love to have seasoned agents, cappers that are like, yeah, hey, let me join up with you. But that's so rare that you wind up with a capper from the blue, out of the blue, coming to a team.

Talk to me about why you love new agents, how you train them, and how that whole situation of everyone sucking at sales has influenced your training.

BRETT

So I just feel like anything I've ever done professionally, when someone tells you how to do it, which is basically the way they did it, and you try to follow that exact method, it just doesn't work. Or it just didn't for me.

Going back, even to, like, when I was a lawyer and I went to law school and we sat in class and did learn millions of things, when I actually got to the job that I had to do, I knew nothing. And it took me actually going up and trying a case and being horrible at it to start getting it in.

AARON

Real estate, our testing is the least useful testing I've ever seen in my life. The training that real estate agents get is just absurd. How many rods in an acre? How many sections in a township? Hurry up. What do you mean you don't know? What's your problem?

BRETT

Right? Yeah. So then I got into real estate, and it was the same type thing people were telling me, sit on the phone, make cold calls, go to open houses every weekend. And it just wasn't working for me. And then one day, it just kind of, like, clicked that I just started doing my own thing, doing almost the opposite of what everybody was telling me, figuring out ways to get into leads and stuff like that that were different from other ways that people did it.

I just got on a roll, and I just kept going and going and going. And that's when I realized, don't listen to whatever anyone else says, don't care what anyone else says, and just figure out what's best for you. And while some things might work best one person, it might not for the other. And then I started, I guess, because I was pretty new at it. I had only done it a couple of years. I felt like hiring newer people that were in the same boat and letting them have free rein of what they thought they were good at and just kind of like pushing them, showing them what I was good at, but not saying, you have to do it that way.

I think things have changed, like, with technology that 20 years ago, the way that one Realtor is doing things that work then, but it might not be the best way to do it now, and that's why I wanted newer people.

AARON

Well, let me ask you about that, because we run trainings. I train my own agents. I train other teams' agents. And there's a couple of things in what you're saying, and I think I hear you, but I want to make sure because there's a difference between do whatever you want and find out what you're good at, because whatever you want.

So let me ask you, I have an agent that only wants to post on social media, even though that's a long-term play and it's not going to bring her any deals next month. And I can't get her to talk to people. A

I think what you're saying is the same thing I say, which is, look, I don't care how you talk to people. You could do it through social media, but it's got to turn into conversations. You could do it through open houses, but it's got to turn into conversations. You could do it by door knocking, cold calling, networking, host parties. I don't care what you do, but you got to talk to people.

BRETT

No, I think what you're saying is right. It has to work, right?

AARON

It's got to work.

BRETT

One particular way isn't enough.

AARON

And I don't do open houses, but everyone on my team does them, and they love them, and I hate them, and I don't do them because I hate them, and I dread going to do it, so I don't do that. But at the end of the day, that three hour, five hour block needs to be used to generate conversations. And if you're not talking to people, you talk to people, there's no help for you. It has to net into a conversation.

BRETT

Yeah. And then I guess so recently, I connected with a social media marketing company to make videos for myself and our team, and it's something I always knew. But right now, the big trend is reels, and people will go on and lip sync ridiculous things and make ridiculous things, and it's funny, and you get likes.

But what they were telling me, and what I also knew, is that really translating into a client calling you up and it's more, you look like an idiot, and you might get some likes.

AARON

How many agents do you have?

BRETT

So I have eight agents. I've slowly added them so they don't all come in at once. Started basically with me and two others and it's now to eight.

We have a transaction coordinator and sales assistant that helps.

I train them a couple of way. Our company does do training, formal trainings. I also can do a formal training and I do here and there. The toughest part is our schedules are all different, so getting everybody together at the same time isn't always easy.

AARON

Do you have weekly meetings or any.

BRETT

Kind of. We were having like every other week but the summer has been a little tough because everybody goes away and stuff like that, but we'll start them again.

Basically anyone on my team knows they can call me at any time. It could be 11:30 at night, it could be seven in the morning. And I believe more in hands on training. Like actually going out and visiting clients, going to a listing appointment, bringing them with, going on any of their showings because when I started and even a lot of companies, they just push this training by sitting either in a live classroom or watching videos and videos and videos. And to me, yeah, you get some knowledge, but half of it you don't use. And then even when you do use it, you still have to see how it applies.

Real people, people are different. Some people are crazy, some people are normal, some people are quiet. So you have to practice. So I believe in just like going taking them to an appointment.

AARON

Fabulous. Ok - first of all, what are the split your splits with them?

BRETT

Yeah, so that's the other thing. When I started real estate, I see all these teams and they come out and I guess it seems like their job is to make a lot of money off of each actual agent on their team. And I guess I didn't want to do that because I wanted to keep them. I want to keep them for forever. If they come to me and say they need more money, we'll discuss it.

And it's not so much me making money off each one. It's more that if I want to go on vacation next week, I have four different people who could pick up, fill in yeah.

And also grow the team so that we're the best team. I generally pay them, like, 70% off the bat, and if they sell a good amount, then we have a discussion and we go up from there.

AARON

Great. And what do they get for their 30%? And that's on top of the compass split, right? That's compass cap.

BRETT

Yeah. So they get me. I'm here all the time. I give them leads, Zillow leads. I get listing leads and I don't believe in, withholding listings from new agents. I think everybody should just go and do everything. They get the CRM that our company gives. But on top of that, I have a CRM. We have a transaction coordinator, a sales assistant who will do anything. She's really good. We have virtual assistants who make phone calls and get leads.

They get everything.

AARON

That's great. That's what they get for the 30%. That's great. Then that's a great starting split in terms of what teams generally offer. And it's certainly on the higher end of what I found to be in terms of a new agent coming in. And then I love the idea of hands on, like, here, let's go do it together. Any agreements they make around lead gen, or is there any production requirements to be on the team? Do people have to do a deal a month?

BRETT

No, there hasn't been yet. No, everybody on the team has been working, but there's no requirement with that.

AARON

Great. And then is there anything that you found hasn't been working or you grapple with? What are the things that keep you up at night around the team?

BRETT

I guess people not working as hard as I work or wanting to be as successful as I want to be. There are some people that come in that are just me, and then there's other people that come in, and they'll work two days a week and be happy with it.

AARON

Yeah. Not everyone wants to be a team leader.

BRETT

Some people just don't want as much, I guess.

AARON

Right. And so culturally, on the team that hasn't shown up for you, like, a problem culturally, like, with other people?

BRETT

No. I mean, everybody's different, so I treat everybody based on what they want, and as long as they're happy, I'm happy.

AARON

Very cool. Yeah. But having people be as interested in succeeding as you are is a really good way to put that. Or even have whatever their definition of success is. Because you get someone who's got two young kids, and their definition of success is at home every day by five and weekends off, and that's their definition of success. And I've certainly interviewed enough team leaders where if that's the person on their team and they want to have a team that has people like that on it, because not every team leader wants people like that on it. But even then, if they do, then it's great.

Any places where you have questions about are you doing it right? Is this the best way to do it? Is there some more efficient way to get this aspect of my team?

BRETT

I don't know. To me, it seems like 90% of people that go into real estate don't stay in real estate very long, from what I hear. To me, you either want to be in it or you don't. And if you're working hard and everything, I'm helping you on top of it. But there's just some people that aren't cut to do it.

AARON

Yeah, well, some people want to sell houses. That's just not what this is.

BRETT

You really can't fight it.

AARON

What do you think your success rate is? Industry standard is like one out of four agents make it kind of thing. Is that about right for your team? Is that about right in your experience over your time, or is there better than that?

BRETT

I could clearly say out of the five that have been here at least like six months, every one of them at least has sold several houses and has potential to stay in this.

AARON

Great. That's great. That's definitely working. That's one of those things that's absolutely working for you, Brett. That's fabulous.

BRETT

I think the main part is with anyone in real estate, when they first get into it, if you're not succeeding within a certain amount of months, you get discouraged and you get out. So my key with me and with everybody is to make you succeed quick.

AARON

That is definitely something that's universal. And the other thing that's universal, Brett, that I've found is the successful teams all have a team leader that have your attitude, which is, I'm here to have my people win. That's your only job is to have them succeed. That's your job. One, it's not your only job, but that's certainly the first job. If you're going to have a team, you got to actually be interested in the person.

It's like selling anything. You got to be interested in the person and what their needs are, what their pain points are and how you can deliver for them. Sounds like that's all rocking. Great. Fabulous. Brett, I appreciate all that because it's exactly the kind of thing that I love to hear about in terms of where other teams are at. Is there anything that I didn't ask that I should have asked you? Is there anything else that you wanted to talk about that I didn't ask?

BRETT

No, I don't think so.

AARON

All right, cool. All right. Well, then the question I always end with is, what are you reading? What should I be reading that I'm not reading or listening to?

BRETT

I don't read much. I'll put that out there. I read so much in law school and college, and I just kind of didn't want to read again. I listened to podcasts like this one because I think it's interesting to hear other people who are doing the same type thing and how they do it because everyone does it. And the way I get so many listings is listening to people. So I run into a book which has nothing to do with real estate, but I kind of like by default.

It actually has helped me. It's called Psychopath Free, and it's about basically some people you think you know how to talk to someone, and certain people have issues that you might not even know, and what they're trying to do is more like manipulate you.

I've run into people who are friends that do it. There are clients that do this. There's other Realtors that do it. And sometimes it's best to just either walk away from these types of people or just if you learn how to handle them, it helps you with the situation, specifically in real estate, and it also makes you a better person.

The book came out of nowhere. I read it. Somebody told me to read it, and it actually has helped with real estate.

AARON

I love it, Brett. That is so good because no one's recommended that book for me.

 **Brett Rosenthal** is an experienced real estate professional in the Greater Philadelphia Area, and a member of the top-producing, award-winning Revolve Philly Group with offices in Center City Philadelphia, Manayunk, Ardmore on the Main Line, Chestnut Hill, and Blue Bell. Brett covers all areas of the City of Philadelphia and the surrounding suburbs, including the Main Line, Bucks County, and Montgomery County.

Brett has received numerous awards and recognition for his sales performance over the last several years. He was recently ranked in Homesnap`s Top 5 Percent Realtors and recognized by Philadelphia Magazine as a top producer in 2022. Brett is a member of the Pennsylvania and Montgomery County Association of Realtors®. Prior to real estate, he worked as a sales executive and manager for a business technology company and was an Attorney where he worked in Real Estate Law for a large NYC Law Firm. Brett received his real estate license in 2015 and focuses on providing home buyers and sellers with professional, responsive, and attentive real estate services. He understands the importance of listening to his clients to find them exactly what they want in a home.

TO CONTACT BRETT

✉ Brett.rosenthal@compass.com

🔗 https://www.revolve-philly.com/
📞 267.342.8001
📷 @topphillyrealtor

PATRICIA LOVE

AARON

Tell us about your back story and your book, *Seen and (Un)Heard*. How has your book made a difference in the world?

PATRICIA

I grew up in Seattle actually. I came from a place of abandonment. My father was unemotional, never around, and didn't know how to hug. He didn't know how to love anybody because of his own issues that I learned about later. My mom was an alcoholic. I was the youngest of three and there were many years between my brother and myself. I was left on my own to do my own thing and was never given any encouragement or inspiration.

I had a roof over my head and food to eat but having a rough up bringing lent itself towards bad behaviors when I was in my teens and twenties. Because I didn't understand how to use the tools I was given and didn't have any guidance or motivation, I went the route of sex, drugs, and rock and roll. It took me a while to recover from that.

I moved out of that phase. I was able to exit and do different things. It's interesting because those behaviors can move into your work life. For example, I've always worked in sales because I wanted to impress my dad. I thought I could earn his love if I copied him and was the best salesperson I could be. I realized later I was sabotaging myself because I was engaging in so many negative behaviors. My mindset wasn't in the right place. I didn't have the tools to understand that this could be different. Can we change? Can I be a millionaire? Can I be a multi-millionaire? Can I be a billionaire? Can I have a balanced life?

Sometimes it can take a lot of trauma before you realize you must make a change. Even though I was highly successful in real estate, I was in the top 5% in the nation. I'm a CRS and have always been in the two few percent, but it was never good enough. I was good at selling real estate and making a lot of money, but I was also good at spending the money because I hadn't changed my negative behaviors in my life. I blamed a lot of people for what happened to me. When my book came out, I realized my story could be anyone's story.

Many women reflected on my stories while regarding their own and realized they can do it too. I can relate to their story as well because I've been through a lot of things. I've lived through deaths and divorces. I was on the hamster wheel that kept producing the same results each time. My goal was to empower women and have women reflect on their own lives to be the best they could be. I didn't change my life until I was 56.

I was successful but that's when the housing market took a dive in 2008. I lost my mom, my husband had left, and I had spent way too much money. I didn't have as much money as I should have in my bank account. When you work in real estate and make commissions, it can be easy to spend because you think you'll just sell another house to make up for it. That's the way it was for me. I was good at it and could always sell another house. Then, everything stopped. I was saved because I had worked in real estate correctly. I hadn't left bodies behind me, I nurtured people. The clients I had sold to 15 years before became my investors.

They would buy investment properties. I turned many of my clients into millionaires because they've owned real estate for a long time and the market has gone crazy. It's a win-win. I was able to maintain my money, but I had to make a lot of behavioral changes because like I said, I was stuck on a hamster wheel and sabotaging myself. Today, I've changed all that. My goal became to help women realize they can and change their behaviors if they are open to it. They must promote their minds to CEO. When people promote their mind to CEO, they start dealing with things and begin to change. People must treat real estate as a business, and many treat it as their hobby. It's not a hobby, it's a business.

CHRISTINE
They act like they will always have business coming to them.

PATRICIA
If people make their real estate their business, that's when the beauty starts to happen. When people change their mindsets, everything opens for them. When I changed my mindset, I changed my negative behaviors I had around finances. I was able to get myself back on top in five years and pay everything off. Now, I'm blessed to say I live a balanced life where I make money and I make passive money through referrals. I made that part of my business plan.

AARON
Can you point to unproductive behaviors you've seen in people and yourself? What do you do as a team leader to empower people on your team to change their unproductive behavior? How can they change themselves.

PATRICIA
People and teams must acknowledge their downfalls, because if I tell them their downfalls, they will get defensive. You must rephrase things for people to understand their own downfalls. I explain if they want to get to a certain point, this is what they need to do. Then, I start working in words of affirmation and add positive words to their vocabularies. If people work positive words into their vocabulary, it becomes habit. I help real estate agents and teams sit down, think about, and write down their negative behaviors. Once they acknowledge their negative behaviors, they can begin to fix them. If they want to be the best in any category, there are things they must do to achieve that. It's a choice they must make.

If someone says they want to make a million dollars this year, that's great, but how are they going to do that? They must create a plan and take baby steps to achieve their goal. In real estate people have such big goals they sometimes forget to take the small steps necessary to achieving the goal. It's not just about them small steps you take to get a client, it's also about the small steps you take to change your mindset on how you get that client.

AARON
What's a small step someone could take?

PATRICIA

The first small step a person could take would be to acknowledge the problem. Because we tend to beat ourselves up in real estate and bring in negative behaviors from our outside life, it's important they forgive themselves for not being perfect or not making 16 deals this month. You can start fresh every day so you can be present and not overwhelmed. People overwhelm themselves too much. Then they paralyze themselves and don't do anything. People will make a list of the things they need to accomplish and continuously put it off until tomorrow. It's important to be present and to only have three to-dos on your to-do list each day. In real estate you must build up your confidence because you will be hit by naysayers and negative people.

The naysayers won't be other real estate agents, they will be new clients who don't know and understand your business and are trying to cut your commission. You feel degraded, so, you must take baby steps to build your confidence. I tell people to write down three easy things they can do in their day and then do a dance a celebrate once they've completed them. That builds confidence. We cannot rely on other people to celebrate us, so you have to reward yourself daily to help build your confidence.

Agents should also hold themselves accountable. When they do that, it's a form of loving yourself, and you continue to preserve. You've checked things off your list and you've done well and you want to do it again tomorrow. The baby steps are taking your through one day at a time. It's like, can the turtle or the ant move the rubber tree plant? The ant moves the rubber tree plant out of sheer persistence.

AARON
Holding yourself accountable is like loving yourself. Why is loving yourself important?

PATRICIA
Because you can't wait to let the outside world tell you how fabulous you are. As much as we would like to receive compliments from our fiends each day, it's a rare thing. It happens sometimes, but people are busy with their own lives. By being accountable and checking off lists, you're really loving yourself. You are creating love for yourself because you are nurturing you. You don't need someone else to hold you accountable because you can hold yourself accountable. If someone wants to help, that's awesome, but it's extra. And so, you don't need, not that you don't want, you don't need somebody else to hold you accountable, because you can hold yourself. Now if somebody wants to, that's awesome, but that's an extra, but it can let your expectations get out of whack.

When you have high expectations and you can't reach them because you're waiting for somebody else to do help you and they let you down, you go into a yo-yo type situation, where your confidence is up and down. In real estate or any kind of commission sales, you must try and be as level as possible on a regular basis, because you may be awesome in your real estate business, but then you take negative things home to your family. You want to be able to balance that out so everybody's happy and it works. It can be done. Nothing is perfect, of course, you're always working on it, but it's so much better to feel at peace at the end of the day, because you did your best and you checked off your list, than to be overwhelmed and feeling badly. When that happens you treat your family poorly because you didn't accomplish what you wanted.

CHRISTINE

Every morning at nine o'clock we have our team members write down five things they can accomplish that have nothing to do with somebody else, so you have that experience of winning.

PATRICIA

That's all it is. It's about winning in your own mind. That's why it's so important to promote your mind to CEOs. Your mind controls you and not enough people utilize their mind. They use it but they aren't using it in the proper way. People must be intentional and use positive words. They must recognize their negative behaviors. Nobody likes to think something is wrong with them. Nobody wants to acknowledge that they might not be good enough. You must bring those behaviors up, because if you don't, you stuff them into suitcases and carry that baggage around with you until the suitcase breaks.

Your baggage could come out in areas you didn't even consider because you didn't deal with you're your issues. I encourage real estate agents, salespeople, and people who work off commission to take time to acknowledge anything negative they may have done or said. Maybe you made a mistake, that's okay. Forgive yourself because you are human. Think about if you had a good mindset all day or if you need to adjust it for tomorrow. Ask yourself if you held yourself accountable and checked the tasks off your to-do list. Ask yourself if you persevered. Did you do your best and not give up? Then you must have a lot of gratitude, because if you don't, it doesn't open the flow to anything else. You're just running after it then.

CHRISTINE

How do you use NLP as a team leader? As an empowerment coach do you use NLP to empower others?

PATRICIA

By using NLP you're empowering yourself, which helps empower others. You're learning the thought processes and mirroring your clients. You're listening to them and trying to understand where they are coming from. Too many people tend to talk and not listen. NLP gives people tools to use to help your clients feel confident. For example, if you client's hands are crossed, you might want to do the same thing. You must listen to what they say and how they say it. It's all about looking at and listening to behaviors. By utilizing NLP with other people, you empower yourself and you help your client relax and feel comfortable with you.

It's all about learning about and understanding people's behaviors. When people see NLP on my resumé they wonder if I'm going to analyze them. It depends on what they are going to do. I might analyze them. NLP is effective because when you listen to them and mimic their actions, you make them feel comfortable and gain their trust. Listening is the biggest part of NLP that is looked over the most. Tapping helps some people but not others. Everybody is different and you must be able to be open to it. Some people think this kind of thing is woo-woo, but I think it's normal. When you're tapping on yourself, you're just hitting on the meridian areas on your body. It helps change the path of your thought process.

Tapping can help people alleviate anxiety because it switches your neuropathways and allows you to refocus.

If people don't like tapping, I give them another exercise that helps refocus their brain. If they feel overwhelmed and refocus their brain on something else, like a pencil, it can help bring down their blood pressure because they aren't overwhelming themselves. They're changing their neuro pathways and calming down.

I always tell real estate agents if they have a situation to not give an opinion or answer right away. Sometimes, we need to step away for two minutes because we need to bring our mind down and our blood pressure lower. Many times, as Wayne Dyer says, "If you change the way you look at things, the things you look at change." in real estate, this is a perfect saying because there's so many ways to get around, do things, and make them work for people. You must have a good mindset while being present. Maybe you're trying to figure out how to get a sale to work and you feel like you've done everything. Maybe you haven't done everything, and you need to step bac and realize that taking a minute will not stop the world. Instead, it will offer you the clarity you need to win that offer.

When people tell me they have anxiety and feel overwhelmed, I tell them to take a step back and pause. I tell them they are going to feel awkward taking a step back, but that it helps. Put the phone down, take your ear plugs out, do anything that will give you peace. Even if you only pause for two minutes, your blood pressure will come down and you'll be able to focus and have clarity on what you need to do. It should become habitual. It's about creating a habit, and the more you do it, the more you get used to it. Now, I do it whenever I'm on the phone and I can feel my blood pressure go up. If you don't want to do tapping, you can do breathing exercises.

If people feel anxious going into a situation, or they are entering a situation with toxic people, I tell them to zip an imaginary bubble around themselves to keep that energy out. I want them to decorate their bubble and realize that no one will be able to penetrate it. Every negative thing will bounce off the bubble. It's a mental exercise, but it works.

CHRISTINE

People think they need to move faster when they need to slow down.

PATRICIA

If you move slower, you will create more energy to move forward, which is critical. When you become more present, you are more at peace with yourself and your transactions. If you're running into people who make you crazy sometimes, just be present and listen to what they are saying. A peace will come over you, and you will still get your work done. In fact, you'll get it done better.

We don't need to answer everything in two seconds. People might think that's how the world should works. Our generation didn't grow up that way though. We didn't work that way, but this is what people know now. People need to be taught the world won't stop if they don't give an answer right away. It will keep going, and they probably won't lose a thing. It's a habit they must get into. I found when they put their phone down, they really have to walk away from the point.

I encourage people to put the phone down, leave it in the house, and take a walk. Even if it's only a two-minute walk to get over the initial fear of not having their phone. Once they get over that, they realize how good it feels. They get feelings of peace and clarity. They can see their goal. Then they make it more of a habit, but they realize that stepping away to think helps get the deal done.

AARON
Is there anything else you would like to add that would make a difference for a team leader or an independent broker when expanding and trying to make their team more effective?

PATRICIA
Teams must work together. It's important to have team meetings in the morning because of the connection and support provided, especially in any kind of commission sales. It's important to leave everybody with something, and many times in real estate, people think they failed when they don't get a deal. If instead they think, "Lessons learned, wisdom earned," the more they can understand these are just lessons. They're gaining wisdom every day, which is fabulous. Words matter. Everything matters. Supporting your team and realizing they have to stop and take a breath sometimes is important.

Patricia Love is the #1 best-selling author of *Seen and (Un) Heard* and founder of the APP ConfidentU. She's a Real Estate Entrepreneur, a Women's Empowerment Coach, a Certified Professional Coach (CPC), and a Practitioner of Neurolinguistic Programming (NLP) and Emotional Freedom Technique (EFT). By combining these practices along with her own personal experience in overcoming real-life challenges and trauma, she's spent the last two decades inspiring and empowering women and girls of all ages to be brave with their story and use their voice for good. While Patricia grew up feeling silenced and misunderstood, she was able to use those experiences as fuel to light her inner fire and make a positive difference in the world around her. She is an advocate for Women's Voices through her "Healing Hoodies" mission.

TO CONTACT PATRICIA

- patricia@patricialove.com
- https://patricialove.com/
- /coachpatricialove
- @coachpatricialove
- @TheRahRahCoach
- /in/lovepatricia/

RYAN GARSON

AARON

Introduce yourself and tell us about your background.

RYAN

I'm an entrepreneur by nature. I started my first business when I was in college. I ran a lot the clubs and bars in Tampa, Florida, where I went to school at USF. I was paid the party. It was awesome. I had a staff of 30 that was made up of all the leaders of the fraternities, sororities, and student organizations. The football team ran my security. I was the Van Wilder of my school. I wish I had it captured on reality TV because there was so much drama. The promoters and the different fraternizes competed, and everyone was hooking up with everyone else. It was a lot of fun, and I was the ringleader.

Then I opened a puppy boutique and franchised it and sold it by the time I was 30. I sold all the boutique items from doggy clothing to strollers. We groomed dogs too. This was in 2005 when having your pet as an accessory was popular. The store was in Boca Raton and was really bougie. After I sold that business, I came to New York City to run a short-term event. It was an art instillation in Columbus Circle near Central Park. When the event ended, they told me I had to run the next event at a fair in Orlando, Florida. This was the first job I ever had, and it was no easy to work for someone else.

I decided I didn't want to run the event in Orlando and stayed in New York City. Then for the next two years I had about eight different jobs. I was working in all kinds of industries. I was working in fashion, helping with events, and working in finance. I was trying to find my path before I got into real estate. Then when I got into real estate, I straight hustled. New York City is very wealthy and prestigious, and I didn't have a Rolodex. My parents weren't handing my deals. I was hustling and doing rentals. I made one sale in my first year and had a couple sales my second year. I did do a ton of rentals, however, which helped me make relationships.

I was networking like crazy and learning the inventory. It's important, especially in New York City, to get familiar with the different buildings and specializing in certain neighborhoods. Now, I've been in business for eight years and have a real estate team of 10. We're going to sell $2 Million in GCI, 60% of which I am going to do. I'm building a team that's producing a lot of revenue and that's new for me. For the last six years I had a small team made up of my cousins and my operations manager.

CHRISTINE
Were you the one slinging all the real estate?

RYAN
I was bringing it in, and my cousin was great at servicing the clients. He's a great copywriter. Then during the pandemic, like most people in New York City, he went to Florida. I ended

up replacing him with three agents while he was going back and forth and networking with people in Miami. When we replaced his roll with three other agents and he was traveling back and forth, that's when it all clicked, so I brought on another sales assistant and a marketing manager too.

Being a real marketing and having a value play differentiated me as an agent. I'm good at marketing because I'm a content creator. Content creators figure out ways to create and distribute content through videos and pictures on social media. I'm working with lifestyle photographers who shoot around the city to shoot at my listings. I make videos about New York City, food, fashion, real estate, and the history of New York City. All that content creation built a following for me on social media and gave me influence.

I would use that influence when going on a listing presentation to get more eyes on what I'm trying to sell. I like to call it new marketing and traditional marketing. Traditional marketing includes taking pictures, writing good copy, and posting it online. Then there is new marketing which includes digital marketing and social media marketing. Every time I create pieces of content, I'll cut it up and use it on all the different social media platforms – LinkedIn, Facebook, Instagram, YouTube, and TikTok. There are a lot of platforms and I'm on all of them. I'm reaching people and getting leads through the content I create.

AARON
Because you are newly in the position of being team leader, do your sales agents do listings or only buyers? Many people start with just buyers, but we couldn't reconcile that on our team.

We told the agents if they brought on a listing, it was their listing.

Talk about the pitfalls you ran into while these guys were doing 40% of your business a year. What was the transition like? What were the problems?

RYAN
I had to let go a little bit and that was difficult for me because I am somebody who wants to do all the steps and service the client the entire way through the process. I had to let go of that. I'm the rainmaker when it comes to bringing in the business, but once the contract is signed our client services representative takes over the deal, so I can move on to the next one. Working a buyer is business. When I'm working a listing, it's a piece of business I am working on. I share that business and we collaborate.

Now I have six sales agents and we all work on business together. We're working on deals and transactions together. We try to get business from our listings. We come up with strategies to get two or three deals from one transaction. We must know how we are going to market ourselves and market the listing. We have different deals going on and everyone has a different personality and their own way of doing business. I must let go a little bit and learn when to lead and when to step away. I'm not a micromanager. I give my guidance and let my team do what they want because we are all independent and entrepreneurial in this business.

I usually come in with a lead or listing and we work it together. My team members will do most of the leg work and then I swoop in and close the deal at the end. We all work together, and we all share the proceeds. One of the pitfalls is figuring out how to work with everybody because there are so many different personalities. It's important to know my team members' strengths and weaknesses, so I know when to collaborate with them.

CHRISTINE

You said that you bring in a deal and you share the proceeds, and they do the leg work. You're the closer and the rainmaker. You're not on a standard 50/50 structure. They're separate. You share deals with them, and they share deals with you. Is that correct?

RYAN

I have six agents and I pick the agent who is the best fit for that deal. My minimum sale is $500,000 and goes up to $4 million. So, they work off commission. Then they can make a money doing rentals in our business. Figuring out who does what is an art form. There is not much structure to it. It's based on how I feel and who I think will produce the best results.

AARON

How much of that 40% were deals they brought in?

RYAN

They brought in about a third of the deals. Many of their deals come from me because I hand them a buyer or put them on my listing. Right now, they are bringing business in, and that's a first for me. In the past I would put them on my listing and give them a percent. Then we would try to work that listing to get more business and convert directs. In New York City you're dealing with buildings, so you can market a whole building and farm and build that way. I'm a farmer. Once I get into a building, I like to really get into a building, and list it in contract. I'll do the quarterly mailers to farm the building. I partner with local coffee shops and give the tenants free coffee. I ramp it up and make sure that I'm doing deals, so I'm known as the man in the building.

CHRISTINE

Tell us about your social media.

RYAN

Real estate is the bread and butter and social media is how I got started. After I started this business, for the first two years I did rentals. Then I started to build my sales during my third year of business. Then during year four, I realized I had a business that worked on buyers and didn't have many listings. Social media was starting to become popular, so I hired a social media manager and influencer who had 100,000 followers and was popular in the makeup and beauty space. She didn't get real estate, so while I learned a lot from her, I didn't feel our message was authentic coming from her.

The posts were too wordy. We worked together for a year and did some good brand building. Then I met an influencer and social media manager who worked for a marketing agency that marketed new developments. I had her take over my social media and this was during the same time that Instagram introduced stories. Then, I started to get some listings. This was my fourth year in real estate, and I sold about seven or eight million dollars in real estate. I was able to make those sales because Instagram stories are such a great way to connect with your followers and your sphere of influence.

Every time I sell an apartment, I connect with them on social media. I'm always trying to get people to follow me on social media, so they can see what I'm doing. Social media is your website and newsletter wrapped into one. People go to you Instagram before they go to your website. Even though I send a monthly newsletter, I still post multiple times a day to social media. It's always at the top of my mind.

For example, one time I shared an Instagram story about the benefits of buying a home. A couple of years ago I met this girl when I first started real estate and we friended each other. We never spoke on the phone after we met, and I didn't have her email address. When she saw my story, however, she sent me a DM that said, "I'm thinking about buying." So, I hopped on the phone with her and sold her a $3 million apartment.

That was when I realized social media was a great way to connect with people who are separated from you by two or three degrees. Then I started to put more time and effort into my social media, and I sold another apartment through a digital ad that I boosted. That was my aha moment when I realized every agent should be marketing and branding themselves on social media. That's when I started Very Social, which is a social media agency that manages social media accounts for brands and entrepreneurs with a focus on real estate agents.

Right now, we have 70 clients, 60 of whom are real estate agents all over the country. We manager their social media for them. We do all the posting for them and create their Instagram stories. We help grow their followers. Many brokers don't have time for social media because they are talking to their clients, running comps, transacting, and running around most of the time. Social media that looks good takes a lot of time and energy to produce. I didn't have the time or the skillset. I knew how I wanted my brand to look and feel, and I have my social media managers convey that look on social media.

Very Social saves our clients time and it elevates their social media presence because we have people who are experts in real estate, design, and copy writing. There are three or four people who touch the content before it goes out, so there are no mistakes. We try to make it seem authentic. Very Social is growing and our clients are staying with us. They're getting business. There are three points to having good social media that stands out. First you need to have good content that will separate you from the rest. If you're only posting what you sold or listed, you're going to bore people.

Your social media needs to be split about 70/30. 70% of the posts should be lifestyle based because that's what people connect with and 30% should be real estate based. People connect with you based on their hobbies, interests, and goals. We work with our clients to help them create content. That's going to engage their followers and get them more business. Second, you must be consistent with social media. You can't post for a week and then take a week off. Your content needs to be consistent. It needs to resonate with your followers. Your social media needs to continue to grow an get bigger, so you have more influence.

CHRISTINE
Do you have packages where you post for the agents? Are you

always going for the brokerage? Are you always going for sales, or do you have social media for recruiting? How varied is it?

RYAN

We can do social media for anyone. Our sweet spot is working with agents or teams that are doing 200,000 to 1,500,000 GCI. Anybody who produces over that has somebody in house doing their social media. Many team leaders don't know if they should focus on the personal or on the team. Their personality needs to come out and shine, otherwise potential clients get bored. If you have to decide between the two, I would say to stick with your personal page. You can have a team page for a professional look and feel and then you can go back and forth and repost things from your personal page to your team page and vice versa. If you're not on social media, you're missing out and you're going to lose to agents who are. Social media marketing and video marketing are the future.

I do a lot of listing videos and when someone comes into see an apartment, they just saw on one of my videos, there is instant rapport and respect. They know who I am. People should be posting videos of their listings to Instagram, TikTok, and YouTube. By doing so, you get on the radar of a potential client. Not only am I posting, I am also advertising it to certain demographics with certain keywords in mind. I post when I have a new listing. I post when it's sold. Social media is something you must keep moving the wheel on to get the most out of it.

AARON

That's what we coach our agents to do on social media. 80%

should be personal and 20% should be business.

RYAN

You can't go wrong with puppy and baby pictures. My two-year-old's on my IG all the time.

AARON

If you go to our YouTube channel, it's only me because I'm the only person on the team making videos.

RYAN

There are so many steps to posting videos on social media. The copy writing, the hashtags, editing and editing the video all take time. Very Social does all that for you. It's a social media manager who is going to work on a day-to-day basis to elevate your social media. It has a strategy in place to make you look good.

CHRISTINE

Will it tell me to make a video and what to say in it?

RYAN

Yes, we do that. We're big into making reels and things for IGTV because we find those to be the most effective. Video is the best way to create conversations on social media. We'll put a storyboard together for you. We'll give you a couple different topics. If you want to do a hot take or a video tour where you interview a local coffee shop owner, we'll give you the outline. Then, you'll shoot the video, and if you need us to, we can source a videographer for a more professional look. Then you get the video to us, we'll edit it for you, and then send it back to you for final approval. Once approved, we post it for you, write the copy, and do the hashtags. If you're a busy real estate agent, let the professionals help you with your social media, because it's a whole other game. If you're spending time working on all the details for your social media, you're missing out on business. You must outsource, so you can do what you're good at.

CHRISTINE

What do your packages range from?

RYAN

They range from $1,000 to $2,000 per month. The price differs based on how many times we post for them. The Get Seen package is $1,000 and that's 12 Indeed posts, 12 Instagram stories, and 12 hours of manual engagement per month. We use your account to look at certain hashtags, geo tags, and popular pages that fit your criteria. We engage with people on your behalf, which grows your followers organically.

Then we have our network of 70 clients comment on your post. When you start, you'll get a minimum of 20 comments per post. Most people don't want to comment if there are no comments, but once there are 20 comments it can go to 30 or 35 quickly. We use our network for engagement, so you're getting more action. The Get Attention package is 16 feed posts, 16 stories, 16 hours of manual growth and 30 comments per month. The Get Attention package, which is $2000 it's 20 feed posts, 20 stories and 20 hours of manual growth and 40 comments per month.

Many agents think their brand is delicate and have a hard time letting it go. If you want to let it go, brokerages don't have anyone to do the work for you. We will do the work for you. You just have to say yes or no. You can tell us where to change the wording. We have the skillset to elevate what you're doing. You only need to communicate with us. It's a collaboration and we're going to make your social media look better. We're going to write good copy, we're going to grow your followers, and we're going to be there along the way to help you create strategy, so you can get business. We want to take your social media to another level that's going to be part of your brand. This should be the most important marketing strategy you have going on right now.

AARON

We put together the Bulletproof Your Business seminar and it encompasses a lot of what you're saying. I doubled my GCI over the pandemic. Prior to that, I had my social media, my past clients, my touch campaigns and all that work. Redfin, Zillow, and Open Door are coming for our business. If you can build a wall like that, Zillow will never be able to touch the connections you make on social media.

RYAN

No, it's all yours. To do social media well and still have time you should have a professional doing it. We get social media. We are doing this for 60 agents. We're a Compass approved vendor. I'd love to be an eXp approved vendor. They can just pay for it right out of their marketing budget. We're here to help. We're here to collaborate with you guys and help grow your brand so you can sell more homes.

There are eight different social media platforms you can be on. You should go with the platform where you feel you can connect to your audience the most and put a strategy in place. Every week I plan for how I'm going to create content and get it out there, so I can sell more houses. Right now is a great time to be in real estate. Social media for real estate agents is interesting because we're advocates for the community and for our clients. People are dependent on us. Real estate is the hottest commodity there is right now. I try to create my own reality show with my social media. My friends and family are into it. I make it entertaining.

That's why 70% of my social media is lifestyle and I sprinkle in the real estate, which is the key information. I don't want to bore them with the real estate stuff. I excite them with me and what I'm doing, but I'm throwing in the market reports, the listings I've sold, stories of how I sold and apartment and stories on how I won a bidding war. That's part of who I am. Being a realtor should be in your social media DNA, but you must make it exciting. I create my own reality show, and I share with everybody on social media and it's part of my brand.

Ryan Garson is a husband, father social media agency founder and real estate agent and team leader living and working in NYC. Ryan is head of the Garson Team, working from NYC to Jersey City, from the Hamptons to Miami and expanding. Over 400 client success stories in the past six years alone. As a seasoned entrepreneur and skilled deal-maker, Ryan is known in the industry for his creative, out-of-the-box approach to marketing. Ryan began Very Social, agency catering to agents over a year ago and the agency has grown by over 400% since January '21!

TO CONTACT RYAN

- ryan.garson@compass.com
- http://garsonteam.com/
- /rgarson
- @ryangsellsnyc
- @RyanGarson
- /in/ryan-garson-9436a917/

NOW WHAT?

Wow!

How inspired are you now? But more than inspired, and even more than motivated, we hope you're ready to act on what you've learned.

There was an awful lot of inspiration in these interviews. And we intended that the information be actionable.

That's why we chose these interviews for this book. These leaders are killing it, and like us, they want to help others do the same.

That was our goal for this book. We've learned that there's a better way to lead a team and run a real estate business, and nothing makes us happier than helping others do that and seeing them succeed like we have. (Okay, maybe having one record-setting month after another makes us pretty happy too…but helping others is pretty awesome)

The fact that you're reading this makes us feel pretty good as well. It means you found the content in this book compelling enough to read all of it.

You now have that information. Do you have the motivation? Are you ready to take your team or brokerage to the next level?

There may have been times you read this book and said, "I didn't know that." We hope that was followed by, "I can do something about that." Because that's our goal for this book. Not to intimidate you, to inspire you. To get you to take action…to take the next step to get to the next level.

One step you can take is reach out to any of the skilled leaders we interviewed. They were happy to share their contact information at the end of their chapter, and they'll be happy to answer your questions about how they got where they are, and how you can learn from that.

And we're here for you as well, to help you learn your own steps for success.

Because you got this book (and have read all of it 😎) we have a really special offer.

We've created a training for our team that is born from what we've learned from our experience and from these team leaders. And if you think it would make a difference for you, and your team, we're happy to open it to you.

At the end of your days, what do you want to say your life fulfilled? What is your calling or purpose in the world, beyond your own income and lifestyle? Can you define it? Do you have an actionable vision for it?

From Grind to Flow: Uncovering Your Life's True North is a guided conversation through a specific framework to help you answer this very question.

We've trained thousands of people over the last 27 years and this is one the most powerful courses we've ever led, and we are delighted to offer it to your team for free.

Book a call with us and let's look at what it could provide for you and your team.

https://calendly.com/aaronhendon/virtualcoffee

Real estate is an amazing profession. It can be incredibly rewarding, and we don't just mean financially. When you become a better leader, you and your team will both do better…in business, and in life. And when your team does better, you do better. If outsourcing some of their training makes sense to you, reach out and let's talk.

To Schedule
From Grind to Flow:
Uncovering Your Life's True North

https://calendly.com/aaronhendon/virtualcoffee

OR TO CONTACT US

🔗 https://christine-and-company.com/

✉ christine@candco.me | aaron@candco.me

📞 206.353.8787

WANT TO PUBLISH A BOOK LIKE THIS?

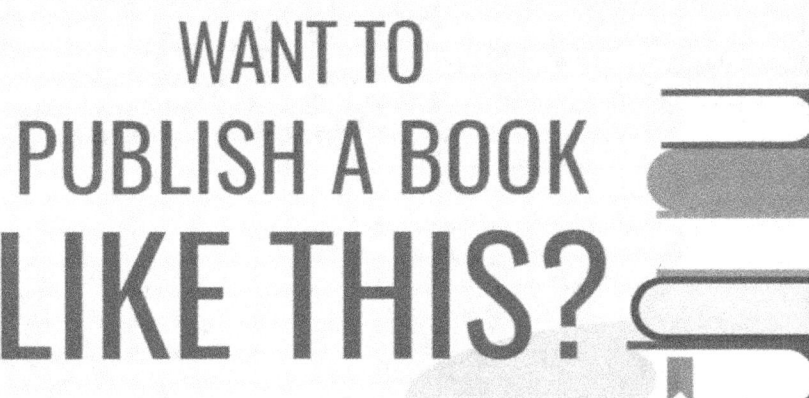

BMD PUBLISHING HAS PUBLISHED DOZENS OF BOOKS LIKE THIS IN NUMEROUS BUSINESS SECTORS.

OUR PROCESS IS EFFICIENT AND EFFECTIVE.

IF YOU'VE ALWAYS WANTED TO DO A BOOK BUT DIDN'T KNOW WHERE TO BEGIN, GO TO WWW.MARKETDOMINATIONLLC.COM/BMDPUBLISHING TO SET UP A FREE *TURN THE PAGE* CONSULTATION.

BEGIN AN EXCITING NEW CHAPTER IN YOUR LIFE!

IT'S YOUR TIME TO BECOME AN AUTHOR

www.ingramcontent.com/pod-product-compliance
Lightning Source LLC
Chambersburg PA
CBHW052348220526
45465CB00003BA/1010